"The Epistle of Christ"

A Report of Meetings
held in Leeds
for four days
April 6th-9th, 1937

Edited by F B Hole

Scripture Truth Publications

"THE EPISTLE OF CHRIST"

Paperback edition first published 1937 by The Central Bible Truth Depot, 5 Rose Street, Paternoster Square, London E.C.4.

Re-typeset and transferred to Digital Printing 2008

ISBN: 978-0-901860-73-6

© Copyright 1937 The Central Bible Truth Depot and 2008 Scripture Truth

A publication of Scripture Truth

All rights reserved. No part of this publication may be reproduced, stored in a retrieval system, or transmitted, in any form or by any means, electronic, mechanical, photocopying, recording or otherwise without prior permission of Scripture Truth Publications.

Scripture quotations, unless otherwise indicated, are taken from The Authorized (King James) Version. Rights in the Authorized Version are vested in the Crown. Reproduced by permission of the Crown's patentee, Cambridge University Press.

Scripture quotations marked "N.Tr." are taken from "The Holy Scriptures, a New Translation from the Original Languages" by J. N. Darby (G Morrish, 1890)

Cover photograph ©iStockphoto.com/ofbeautifulthings (Tim Robbins)

Published by Scripture Truth Publications
31-33 Glover Street, Crewe, Cheshire, CW1 3LD

Scripture Truth is an imprint of Central Bible Hammond Trust, a charitable trust

Typesetting by John Rice
Printed and bound by Lightning Source

"THE EPISTLE OF CHRIST"

Editor's Foreword

On each of the four days a Bible Reading was held in the morning, an Open Meeting in the afternoon, and in the evening various speakers were invited by the local brethren to give Addresses.

The passages before us in the Readings were chosen as giving the mind of the Lord for us during the time of His absence: (1) as made known to His disciples before He left them; (2) as disclosed in His prayer to the Father; (3) as made known by Him through the Apostle Paul; and (4) through the Apostle John. The reports of these Readings are printed together at the beginning of the book so that their continuity may be the better preserved.

The Addresses follow in the order in which they were delivered. The Contents list indicates the meeting in which each was given, and the speaker. If this be noted, any allusion made here and there to the remarks of some previous speaker will be quite intelligible.

No attempt has been made to produce a verbatim report. In the Readings no speakers are shown, questions have been omitted, the answers having been incorporated into the general summary of what was said. The Addresses have been revised and condensed by the various speakers. The whole has finally been revised by the Editor, with a view to producing it in as convenient and compact a form as possible.

Those present at these meetings were conscious of the Lord's guidance and blessing. This little book is issued with the prayerful desire that many who were not present may share, to some extent at least, in the blessing.

F. B. Hole

"THE EPISTLE OF CHRIST"

"THE EPISTLE OF CHRIST"

CONTENTS
BIBLE READINGS
Fruit-bearing and Testimony 7
The Prayer 14
The Walk Worthy of the Calling 22
Philadelphia and Laodicea 32

ADDRESSES
AFTERNOON MEETING – DAY 1
The Head of the Church . . . . *W. Blakeborough*   42
Antecedents to Assembling together . . . . *T. Oliver*   46

EVENING MEETING – DAY 1
Our Wealth—our Walk . . . . *W. Bramwell Dick*   52
Christ, the Pattern of the Christian Life
. . . . *Hamilton Smith*   59

AFTERNOON MEETING – DAY 2
Riches from God's Treasury . . . . *W. C. Reid*   67
"His Fulness" . . . . *G. Davison*   72

EVENING MEETING – DAY 2
A Word on Service . . . . *R. McCallum*   76
The Seven Words . . . . *J. T. Mawson*   84

AFTERNOON MEETING – DAY 3
Encouragement for Closing Days . . . . . . *J. Houston*   90
"An Everlasting Light" . . . . *A. Steiner*   96

EVENING MEETING – DAY 3
Unity from Above . . . . *A. J. Pollock*   99
The Cross of Christ . . . . *F. B. Hole*   104

"THE EPISTLE OF CHRIST"

AFTERNOON MEETING – DAY 4

Lord and Christ .... *R. Nelson*   112

The Path of Obedience .... *C. N. Snow*   117

Christ's Building and ours .... *A. F. Pollock*   122

EVENING MEETING – DAY 4

Christ, the Object: His constraining Love, the Power
.... *J. Houston*   126

The Knowledge of the Son of God ...... *D. Ross*   130

"The Epistle of Christ" .... *Hamilton Smith*   136

Fruit-bearing and Testimony
BIBLE READING ON JOHN 15:1-17

The great truth that underlies the teaching of the last discourses would seem to be that it is God's desire that, when Christ personally is gone back to the glory, Christ morally should still be seen in His people. In other words, that, as the disciples of Christ, believers should be in this world to represent Christ.

Chapters 13 and 14, are introductory to this end. In chapter 13, we find that we are to have part with Christ in His things where He is. This leading thought is expressed in the Lord's words "*part with Me*" (13:8). In chapter 14, the Lord speaks of the coming of the Spirit, and as a result it will be possible for the Lord to have *part with us* (14:21-23). These two things are beautifully expressed in the Lord's touching appeal, in the address to Laodicea, when He says, "If any man hear My voice, and open the door, I will come in to him, and will *sup with him*, and *he with Me*." It shows that in the last days it is possible to get back to the Lord's teaching at the beginning.

The discourses of chapter 13, and 14, take place in the Upper Room, and the truths unfolded prepare the disciples for the outside place of testimony. At the end of chapter 14, the Lord says, "Arise, let us go hence." Immediately they pass from the privacy of the Upper Room to the public street, and the truths connected with testimony before the world begin to be unfolded.

The leading truths of chapter 15, are fruit-bearing and testimony. That which goes up to the Father as fruit will go out to the world as testimony.

In verses 1 to 8, the Lord instructs us as to fruit-bearing.

In verses 9 to 17, we have a lovely description of the new Christian company in which fruit is found.

In verses 18 to 25, we learn that the opposition and hatred of the world will be aroused by a company of disciples that set forth the character of Christ.

In verses 26, and 27, we hear of the power of the Spirit that will enable the disciples to witness for Christ in the world that hates Christ.

Fruit is the reproduction of the character of Christ in His people. Galatians 5:22 gives a beautiful description of fruit, or, in other words, the character of Christ. There we read, "The fruit of the Spirit is love, joy, peace, long-suffering, kindness, goodness, fidelity, meekness, self-control" (N.Tr.). Fruit, as presented in the fifteenth of John, is not preaching or teaching, or other forms of service. Were it so, fruit would be confined to the few who have gifts. Fruit is possible for every one, the youngest as well as the oldest; and where there is no fruit the branch is taken away.

Of all trees the vine is chosen because it is the one tree that is perfectly useless unless it bears fruit. Ezekiel, speaking of the vine, asks, "Shall wood be taken thereof to do any work? or will men take a pin of it to hang any vessel thereon?" (Ezekiel 15:2-5).

We have to keep out of the passage the truth of the Head and the Body; otherwise we might be led to think that a true believer can be cut off from Christ. Here it is a question of those who profess to be the disciples of Christ. The life is in the vine and in every true branch there is life flowing from the vine, and this life manifests itself in fruit. But the figure speaks of withered branches and thus leaves room for a lifeless profession. The Lord goes on to show the means used in order that the branches that bear fruit may bear "more fruit" and "much fruit".

First we have what the Father does that we may be fruitful. The Father is the Husbandman, and "every branch that beareth fruit He purgeth it, that it may bring forth more fruit." Do we not get this gracious work brought before us in Hebrews 12:6-11, where we read of the Father's dealing with His children that they may be partakers of His holiness?

Secondly, in verse 3, we have the Lord's work to the end that we may bear fruit. He applies His word to the conscience and heart in order to remove every defilement that would hinder the development of fruit. Is not this the feet-washing of chapter 13?

Thirdly, there is what we ourselves do,—our responsibility to abide in Christ, in order that we may bear fruit.

Abiding in Christ implies a walk in constant dependence upon, and loving communion with, the Lord. Alas! we can preach and teach and be very active in service, even when out of touch with the Lord, as was the case with the Corinthian saints, and with some of whom the Apostle said, they "preach Christ even of envy and strife"; but to wear the beautiful character of Christ will only be possible as we are in the company of Christ. In the matter of bearing fruit, the Lord's words are ever true, "Without Me ye can do nothing."

Verse 6 proves that the figure sets forth profession, which may be real or lifeless. Judas would appear to be a solemn example of one who made a profession of being a disciple, but, having no life, brought forth no fruit, and was "cast forth". Verse 2 would seem to be rather different. The figure seems to contemplate a branch with life but no fruit. Possibly it answers to those that we read of in 1 Corinthians 11:30, who, though believers, were walking so badly that they brought forth no fruit, and were taken away. In verse 2, we have a fruitless believer, in verse 6, a lifeless professor. In the first case we read, "He taketh it away"; in the second case the dead branch is "cast forth".

In verses 7 and 8, we have the results of bearing fruit. First, as to ourselves; if abiding in Christ, and thus bearing fruit, we shall ask according to the mind of the Lord, and our prayers will receive an answer.

Secondly, if bearing fruit, the Father will be glorified. In all that Christ was, and said, and did, He displayed the Father. It follows that if we set forth anything of the character of Christ, in that measure we shall go forth, and glorify, the Father.

Thirdly, if bearing fruit, and thus setting forth the character of Christ it will become manifest before the world that we are the disciples of Christ. The character of Christ in believers, that goes up to the Father as fruit, will go out to the world as testimony.

In the verses that follow (9 to 17), we have the marks of the new Christian company in which alone fruit will be found. It is obvious that many of the beautiful qualities of Christ, such for instance as kindness, gentleness and longsuffering, could hardly be set forth by an isolated individual. It requires a company to set forth the loveliness of Christ.

The first great mark of the Christian company is that they are loved by Christ. Even as the Lord walked through this world in the consciousness of the Father's love, so He would have us to face all the opposition and hatred of this world in the consciousness that the love of Christ is ever streaming down upon us.

They are to be characterized also by obedience. "If ye *keep* My commandments, ye shall abide in My love." Again, the Lord is the perfect pattern of this beautiful quality. Walking in the sunshine does not make the sunshine, but it leads to the enjoyment of the sunshine. So obeying His commands does not draw out the Lord's love but it leads to the enjoyment of the love.

The next mark is "joy". But it is the Lord's joy; may we not say the joy of the Father's love? Abiding in the love of the Lord we should be walking in the joy of the Lord. This joy is to remain *in* us. It is not the joy of the world that depends on outward circumstances. David can say, "Thou hast put gladness *in my heart*, more than in the time that their corn and their wine increased" (Psalm 4).

Then the Lord desires that the new company should be a *loving* company. They are, indeed, loved by the Lord; but they are to love one another. The love to one another received its greatest expression when Christ died for His friends.

This new company is also one that the Lord takes into His confidence and treats as His friends. We are, indeed, privileged to be His servants, but the Lord treats us not as servants merely, to whom the Master would speak only concerning their work, but as friends to whom the Master confides the inmost thoughts and purposes of His heart. Thus, treating His disciples as friends, the Lord says, "*All things* that I have heard of My Father, I have made known unto you."

The next mark is that they are a company "chosen" by the Lord. It would be no wonder if we had chosen Him; it is a great wonder that He should have chosen us. Having chosen us He will never give us up. Here it is that we have been chosen to bring forth fruit, and that our fruit should remain. We are "set" (N.Tr.)—not "ordained"—each in our place to set forth Christ, and all that is of Christ; and only what is of Christ in us, will remain.

Lastly, they are to be a praying company, and thus dependent upon the Father, that "whatsoever ye shall ask of the Father in My name, He may give it you."

To sum up the Lord's desires for His people, as unfolded in this great passage, we may say that the Lord would have such,

> First, to be walking in the consciousness of His love;
>
> Secondly, to obey His commands;
>
> Thirdly, to have His joy in them;
>
> Fourthly, to love one another;
>
> Fifthly, to be in His confidence as His friends;
>
> Sixthly, to realize that they are chosen to bring forth fruit;
>
> Seventhly, to be dependent upon the Father as a praying people.

It will be noticed that in all these lovely marks there is a total absence of the things in which the flesh seeks to exalt

FRUIT-BEARING AND TESTIMONY

itself. For anyone to seek distinction in this company by boasting in birth, or social position, or riches, or intellectual attainments would be to introduce elements of this world that at best could only be possible for the few, and would mar the unity of the company. All the marks of this new company are moral, and as such can be enjoyed by the youngest believer as well as the oldest.

Here, then, we have the desires of the Lord for the whole Christian company, and any little local company of believers having these marks, will bear fruit for the Father and be, in their little measure, a testimony before the world. Let us remember that, however great the corruptions of Christendom, it is still possible for any company of believers to have these marks, for they are all moral, and call for no exercise of miraculous power. Nevertheless they accomplish something far greater for they set forth the loveliness of Christ.

The Prayer

BIBLE READING ON JOHN 17

That we are privileged to hear the Son speaking to the Father in prayer, gives to this portion of the Word its unique character.

In the first part of the prayer the Lord expresses His desires for Himself (verses 1 to 5); in the second portion the Lord prays, more especially, for His disciples who had accompanied Him on earth (6 to 19); in the last portion the Lord prays for all those who would believe on Him, through their word (20 to 26).

There would seem to be three great desires underlying the prayer; First, that the Father may be glorified in the Son (verse 1); secondly, that Christ may be glorified in His people (verse 10); thirdly, that His people may be glorified with Him (verse 22).

In Scripture "glory" conveys the thought of exalting a person through bringing into display all the excellences that distinguish that person. In John 13:31, we read, "Now is the Son of Man glorified, and God is glorified in Him." This verse takes us to the cross, and that aspect of the cross, wherein every excellence of the Son of Man was displayed under the supremest test and all the glory of God was upheld. The following verse takes us to the glory. The Son of Man, having glorified God on the cross, is Himself glorified on high and that immediately. Thus, the excellencies of the Son of Man are brought into display both at the cross and in the glory.

In the prayer the first request is that the Father would glorify the Son; but, even so, it is that the Son may use this new place of exaltation to glorify the Father, as He had already glorified the Father by setting forth His excellences on earth. The natural man seeks to glorify himself; here, at last, we see One who seeks to be glorified *by* the Father, in order that He may bring glory *to* the Father.

With this object in view, authority had been given to the Son over "all flesh", that He might give eternal life to as many as the Father had given to Him. It was no longer authority given to Christ as the Messiah in connection with the Jews, but the far wider authority over all flesh—Jew and Gentile alike. Moreover the blessing has in view, not simply a godly Jewish remnant but that far greater company that embraces all believers given by the Father to the Son.

In verses 4 and 5, three great facts pass before us which are the everlasting basis of all our peace and blessing. First, the Lord says, "I have glorified Thee on the earth." This brings out the perfection of His Person. In the very world where men had dishonoured God there has been One who, in the most absolute way, glorified God.

Secondly, the Lord can say, "I have finished the work that Thou gavest Me to do." This takes us to the cross and tells us that all that the Father gave Him to do, to uphold the glory of God and secure the blessing of men, has been done.

Thirdly, the Lord asks to be glorified in the glory, and thus in this new place to become the everlasting proof of God's satisfaction with Himself and the work He accomplished.

In the course of the prayer we notice, as throughout the Gospel of John, that the glory of the Son, as a Divine Person, is ever kept before us; while, at the same time, the Lord never moves out of the place of Servant that He had taken as Man, and therefore He is ever the receiver and the Father the giver.

We see the glory of His Person shine out in a special way in verse 5. A man might, indeed, desire to be glorified; but who, that is only man, could add the words "With Thine own self". We might desire to be glorified with the saints, but only a Divine Person could ask to be glorified with a Divine Person. It is still more manifest that none but a Divine Person could use the words, "With the glory which I had with Thee before the world was".

With verse 6 we pass on to the portion of the prayer in which the Lord prays for His disciples. First, however, the Lord recalls His work in the midst of His own (verses 6 to 8); and presents the great motives for His prayer (9 to 11).

While with the disciples the Lord had manifested the Father's name to them, and had made known to them the Father's words. Moreover, the Lord utters no word as to their failure and ignorance that the history so often reveals, but credits them with so much that is beautiful. The Lord can say, "They have *kept* Thy word"; "They have *known*"; "they have *received*"; and "they have *believed*".

Then, in verses 9 to the middle of verse 11, we have the record of the great motives for the prayer.

The Lord says, "They are Thine." He is praying to the Father about those who *belong to the Father*.

Again, the Lord pleads that those for whom He prays are *His own*, and He is glorified in them.

Then the last motive for the prayer is connected with the disciples themselves and *their needs*, for the Lord can say, "I am no more in the world, *but these are in the world*, and I come to Thee."

With the middle of verse 11, we come to the first great request on behalf of His own:—"Holy Father, keep through Thine own name those whom Thou hast given Me." Name, in Scripture, sets forth what a person is. "Holy Father" speaks of all that the Father is in holiness and love. The request is that the disciples may be kept in consistency with the holiness and love of the Father. Peter, in his Epistle exhorts all who "call on the Father" to be holy even as He is holy (1 Peter 1:14-17). It was only the Son, who ever dwelt in the bosom of the Father, who could "declare" the Father. Abraham and Moses could speak of the attributes of God as the Almighty, and as Jehovah, but none but a Divine Person could reveal the Father's heart and declare the Father's Name.

The next request is conveyed in the Lord's words, "That they may be one as we." The Father and the Son were ever perfectly united in purpose and object. The service of the disciples may take many different forms, as we see in the different ministries of Peter, John, and Paul, but the Lord desires that they may all be perfectly united in having the same purpose and object that is ever before the Father and the Son.

In the verses that follow the world is viewed as opposed to the Father, and hating all that belong to the Father, whether Christ, or His people, so the next request of the Lord is that the disciples may be kept from the evil of the world (verse 15). If Christ is to be glorified by being represented in His people they must be apart from the evil of the world.

Then comes the desire that they may be sanctified (17-19). If we are to be witnesses for Christ, it is not enough that we are kept from evil, we must also be sanctified; and this implies that we are not only set apart *from* evil, but are set apart in heart and life *to* and *for* Christ. It brings in the thought of devotedness to the Lord. There are many things which may not be evil, and yet from which we should be wholly apart if devoted to the Lord.

The Lord indicates two ways in which this practical sanctification can be brought about. First, the Lord's words are, "Sanctify them through Thy truth; Thy word is truth." The truth instructs us in the mind of the Lord and engages our hearts with that which leads to a devoted life. Secondly, the Lord adds, "I sanctify Myself, that they also might be sanctified through the truth." By engaging our hearts with Himself in the glory—the One in whom perfect devotedness has been set forth, as well as the end to which it leads, we become "changed into the same image from glory to glory".

In the portion of the prayer that follows, the Lord embraces in His requests all that would believe through the word of the Apostles — believers of the church period. While, however, we distinguish the two portions of the prayer, it would surely be as wrong to *confine* the earlier requests to the disciples present with the Lord, as to *exclude* them from the later requests. The words of the Lord, "Neither pray I for these alone", would indicate that the desires already expressed by the Lord equally apply to all believers, while the last requests, by their very nature, must include the disciples who were with Him then.

In verse 21 the request is that believers, "all may be one", and the Lord adds "one in us". This then is a unity in their common interest in Christ, and in communion with the Father and the Son. This unity was to be a witness to Christ before the world: "That the world may believe that Thou hast sent Me." If the world could see a company of people who, though sharply divided by nationality, or wealth, or social position, are yet all bound together by their common interest in Christ it would be to them an arresting witness to the power of Christ. For a short time it was so when, at the beginning, the world saw with amazement that "the multitude of them that believed were of *one heart* and *one soul*". From a people thus united in their common interest in Christ there went out a witness to the world of "great power" and "great grace" (Acts 4:32, 33).

Then, the Lord, having viewed believers in their mission in this world, as His sent ones to represent Himself, now looks on to the coming glory and prays that, "they may be one, even as we are one: I in them, and Thou in Me". This is the third unity for which the Lord prays in the course of the prayer. The first is a unity in object—"One as we"; the second, is a unity in common interest in Christ and communion with Divine Persons—"One in us"; the third unity is a unity in the glory of the Kingdom when all believers will be "perfected into one" (N.Tr.). Then, indeed, Christ will be seen in the saints, even as the Father is seen in the Son. When the Lord appears He will be "glorified in His saints" and "admired in all them that believe". The world will then know that the Son was sent by the Father, and that the Father loved believers, even as the Father loved the Son.

The last request carries us beyond the Kingdom glories into the yet greater privileges and deeper blessedness of the Father's home: — "I will that they also, whom Thou hast given Me, be with Me where I am". It was wonderful grace that brought the Lord Jesus down to be with us where we are; it is yet more wonderful that He should take us up to be with Him where He is.

We are not yet with Christ in the Father's home, so in the closing verses the Lord clearly indicates our present portion, and the purpose for which we are left in this world. The final words, "*I in them*" tell us once again that the great purpose that underlies the last instructions of the Lord to His disciples, as well as the prayer to the Father, is that His people should in word and acts, and manner of life, represent Him during the time of His absence. With this great end in view we may well ponder, and seek to answer to these great requests of the Lord:—

> First, that we may walk in consistency with the holiness and love of the Father;
>
> Secondly, that we may be united in having one object and purpose before us—the glory of Christ;
>
> Thirdly, that we may be kept from the evil of the world, in order to be a true witness to Christ;
>
> Fourthly, that we may be sanctified, or devoted to Christ and His interests;
>
> Fifthly, that, forgetting the things that are behind, we may be united in our common interest in Christ and in communion with Divine Persons;
>
> Sixthly, that we may be one in the coming Kingdom to display the glory of Christ and the love of the Father;

Seventhly, that at last we may be with Christ in His own home—the Father's home, for the delight of His heart.

Such is the mind of Christ for His people as expressed to the Father, in our hearing, in this last great prayer. Answering to His mind we should truly represent Him and thus His words would have their answer:—"I IN THEM".

The Walk Worthy of the Calling
BIBLE READING ON EPHESIANS 4:1-16

There is a connection between this passage and John 15, and 17, that we have been considering, inasmuch as the ministry by which the Lord makes known to us His mind cannot be confined to His personal communications to His disciples, or the great prayer to the Father. There are also the revelations made to us through Paul and the other Apostles. In this passage we have a summary of the truths communicated through the Apostle Paul, and the practical application of these to our walk.

In the last discourse the Lord said to His disciples, "I have yet many things to say unto you, but ye cannot bear them now." He thus indicates that further truth would be communicated from Himself by the Spirit. In this Epistle we have the revelation of the highest truth as to the church and its heavenly calling.

The "calling" includes all the spiritual and heavenly blessings that believers are called to enjoy, and which were purposed for them before the foundation of the world. This calling is unfolded to us in chapter 1. The way God has wrought, in time, to bring this calling to pass, comes before us in chapter 2. In chapter 3, we learn the right condition of soul—Christ dwelling in the heart by faith—in order that we may enter into the truth of the calling.

In connection with the calling of God we have not only the blessings into which we are called as individuals, as unfolded to us in chapter 1, but also the further great truth that believers are viewed corporately as the Body of Christ, and collectively as the House of God (1:22-23; 2:20-22; 3:4-6). In connection with this truth two expressions are used which would indicate God's purpose in them. In connection with the Body we have the expression "the fulness of Christ" (1:23; 4:13); thus indicating that in the one body there is to be set forth all the moral excellencies—the fulness—of Christ the Head. Then in chapter 3:19 we have the expression "the fulness of God", which would seem to be used in connection with the House of God, implying that in believers, viewed as the House of God, there should be the setting forth of the fulness of God in His love, and grace, and holiness. In order that these things may be set forth in the saints, the Apostle begins to speak of the practical walk that is worthy of this high calling.

In verse 1, we are exhorted to a walk worthy of our calling.

In verses 2 and 3, there are set before us the beautiful qualities that constitute a worthy walk.

In verses 4 to 6, we have three different circles in which this worthy walk is to be manifested.

In verses 7 to 16, we have in greater detail, the walk, and the gracious provision for this walk, in connection with the first circle—the sphere of the Spirit (verse 4).

In verses 17 to 32, we have the walk consistent with the second circle under the authority of the one Lord.

In chapters 5 to 6:19, we have the walk that becomes those who own the third circle, in which there is "one God and Father". This naturally brings in all the relationships of life.

The Epistle closes with exhortations as to the conflict that will be entailed in seeking to maintain the truth of the calling and to walk in the light of it (6:6-20).

Coming back to the verses we have read, our thoughts are confined more especially to the walk that is consistent for believers as members of the one body. This walk is summed up in seven beautiful qualities in verses 2 and 3—lowliness, meekness, longsuffering, forbearance, love, unity, and peace. These qualities set forth the loveliness of Christ.

There is a difference between "lowliness" and "meekness". "Lowliness" has reference to myself. "Meekness" has reference to my brother. "Lowliness" would lead to low thoughts of self; "meekness" would lead to giving way to others in things relating to self.

If rightly apprehended, the first great effect of the truth of the calling, would be "lowliness", or to give us low thought of ourselves. As the House of God we are built together for an habitation of God through the Spirit. The sense of being in the presence of God, would lead to lowliness. In chapter 3, we are told how the Apostle when he found himself in the presence of " the unsearchable riches of Christ", "the manifold wisdom of God" and "the eternal purpose", at once confesses that he is "less than the least of all saints".

In seeking to understand a word it is often helpful to think of its contrast. Haughtiness would seem to be the opposite of lowliness. Self-assertiveness, the opposite of meekness. The mere intellectual apprehension of a truth would only lead to knowledge that puffs up. The same truth seen in the presence of Christ would lead to lowliness, for in His presence we feel how small we are.

If we live up to the truth of the calling, it may lead us into a position like Paul. Not only had he to suffer imprisonment, but there arose an occasion when he had to say, "All men forsook me." We may not be called to go to prison, but it shows that the more clearly we confess the truth, and live in consistency with it, the more we shall be in reproach down here.

But insults, reproaches, and desertions, call for longsuffering and forbearance, the next qualities of which the Apostle speaks. Nevertheless in our longsuffering we need care. In the presence of insults we may be silent and show great forbearance, and yet it may spring from the pride that treats an offender with silent contempt. We are therefore exhorted to exercise forbearance toward "one another in love". It may be right to be silent in the presence of insults, but let it be the silence of love. In the presence of such insults as we have never been called to meet, the Lord was silent with a love that could pray for the man that spat in His face. "Father, forgive them; for they know not what they do."

Any effort to keep the unity of the Spirit apart from these qualities must fail. Doubtless here, as in other Scriptures, there is a divine order in the way these moral qualities are presented. To keep the unity of the Spirit we surely need the condition of soul implied by lowliness, meekness, longsuffering, forbearance, and love.

The unity of the Spirit is the one mind of the Spirit. We may arrive at one mind by common agreement and yet entirely fail to have the mind of the Spirit, and thus fail to keep the unity that His mind would produce. The unity of the Spirit cannot be arrived at by agreement or compromise, but by each seeking to have, and endeavouring to act according to, the mind of the Spirit. On the one hand, it is evident that nothing that we can do can alter the mind of the Spirit; in this sense we cannot break it. On the other hand we may fail to act in accord with His mind, and thus fail in keeping the unity that His mind would produce.

If two brothers do not see eye to eye, it is evident that one, or both, have not the mind of the Spirit, and the danger is that they will fall to quarrelling; and strife leads to division. Therefore, when there is a divergence of judgment we are warned not to press our own judgment, but each to seek to arrive at the unity of the Spirit in the bond of peace. Strife tends to divide; but peace unites. Therefore the word speaks of "the uniting bond of peace" (N.Tr.).

If we ask, what is the mind of the Spirit? we may surely say it is expressed in the seven "ones" of verses 4 to 6,— one body, one Spirit, one hope, one Lord, one faith, one baptism, and one God and Father of all. The whole circle of Christian truth is connected with these unities that the Spirit is here to maintain; and it is only as we seek to enter into them that we shall arrive at the mind and unity of the Spirit.

A right condition of soul—the lowly mind of Christ—is necessary in order to enter into these things. For this reason, after having unfolded some of these great truths in the early part of the Epistle, the Apostle concludes the third chapter with prayer. He seems to say—There is nothing left for me but to get on my knees and pray that you may be strengthened with might by the Spirit, in the inner man, so that Christ may dwell in your hearts, that you may "comprehend", and "know", and be "filled" with all the fulness of God.

There are three circles described in these verses. The first marked by the Spirit; the second by the authority of the Lord; and the third flowing from the great truth that there is one God and Father of all. In the first circle—the vital circle—everything is real. In Christendom we see how every one of these great truths has been set aside. The various sects are a denial that there is one body; human arrangements and organizations have set aside and ignored the presence of the Holy Spirit; and Christendom has settled down to earth and sought to use Christianity merely as a means to make this world a better place, thus setting aside the truth of the heavenly calling.

The second circle includes all that profess the Lord. The verse supposes such to be real, for every true believer owns the Lordship of Christ. Nevertheless it is possible to profess the Name of the Lord, the faith of Christianity, and submit to Christian baptism without personal faith in Christ, and thus the verse leaves room for the vast profession of Christendom.

The third circle is the largest circle of all. It is the creation circle, in which there is "One God and Father *of all*", who is "*above all*", and "*through all*", and "*in us all*" (N.Tr.). As the Creator, God is the source of all. Then we have a truth of immense comfort. Whatever power of evil we have to meet, God is "above all"; whatever circumstances we may be called to pass through, God is working out His plans "through all"; and, moreover, as far as believers are concerned, He is "in us all", as we read in chapter 3:20, He "worketh in us". We are reminded too of the beautiful passage in Isaiah, where the prophet says, "When thou passest *through* the waters, I will be with thee; and *through* the rivers, they shall not overflow thee; when thou walkest *through* the fire thou shalt not be burned; neither shall the flame kindle upon thee" (Isaiah 43:2).

Walking in the truth of the first circle would put us outside all the systems of men, and keep us in unity. Walking in the truth of the second circle would bring us under the authority of the Lord, and shut out the principle of independency of assemblies which is a practical denial that there is one Lord. Walking in the truth of the third circle would bring us, as the children of God, to "walk in love" and shut out all unholiness and malice (5:1-3). To get back to these great truths and seek to walk in the light of them is to learn the one mind of the Spirit, and to endeavour to keep the unity of the Spirit.

Passing on to verses 7 to 16, the Apostle shows the provision that is made in order that believers may walk consistently with the truth that they form the body of which Christ is the Head—the circle described in verse 4. In the course of these verses we learn there is that which is given to "every one" for the good of the body (verse 7); then, there are the gifts given to "some" (verse 11); finally, there is that which is ministered directly from the Head, through the members of the body, viewed, not as individuals, but as "fitly joined together" (verse 16).

There has been some difference of thought as to the exact interpretation of verse 7. Is not the Apostle showing that there is a service committed to every believer, as distinct from the gifts that are given to "some"? That it should be given to us to serve Christ in any form is a great "grace", and therefore the service is referred to as "grace". This grace, however, is given in different measures according to the sovereign gift of Christ. We might be inclined to think that if we have no special gift we have nothing to do for the Lord. The verse would indicate that we all have some little service for Christ. Romans 12:6 to 8, as well as other Scriptures, clearly shew that there are many forms of service such as "giving", "leading" and "shewing mercy", beside the specific gifts.

Having spoken of what is given to "every one", the Apostle passes on to speak of the gifts that are given to "some" (verses 8-11). The gifts come from the Risen Head as the token of His victory over every adverse power. It has often been noticed that in this list of gifts there is no mention of the sign gifts—the gifts of tongues and healing. Sign gifts were given at the beginning as a testimony to the world, and perhaps more especially to the Jew. In spite of these signs the Jew has entirely rejected the testimony to Christ in the glory, and the Church has entirely failed in its responsibility to give a united witness to the world. Hence, it would seem that these gifts have been withdrawn.

Moreover, in this passage the Apostle is speaking of the inside circle—the edifying of the body. Here the sign gifts, which were a testimony to the world, would have no place. Paul exercised the gift of healing as a testimony to the world, but, apparently, never used this gift in the circle of the saints; as it has been pointed out, he never healed his friends.

The fact is emphasised that the Lord "descended first", for had we simply the statement that "He ascended", we might have been left wondering whether He had triumphed over every adverse power. But we are told that He went first to the lowest point, and from the lowest place has ascended to the highest, and thus overcame every enemy from the lowest to the highest.

In the primary sense of the words we no longer have Apostles and prophets; though we must remember that in an important sense these gifts are still with us, since we have the benefit of their ministry in a permanent form in the Holy Scriptures.

Having spoken of the gifts the Apostle proceeds to speak in verse 12 of the threefold purpose of the gifts. First, they are given "for the perfecting of the saints". This would be the establishment and spiritual growth of the saints individually. Secondly, they are given for "the work of the ministry". This would include evangelising by which the gospel is carried out to the world. The third great end of the gifts is "the edifying of the body of Christ". Whether it is the perfecting of the saints individually, or preaching the gospel to sinners, we are ever to keep before us that all is in view of the edifying of the body of Christ.

In verse 13 we learn more definitely what is meant by "the perfecting of the saints". The Apostle does not refer to the perfection of the resurrection state, which would include the change of the body, nor of what some speak of as "sinless perfection". The perfection is that of a "full-grown" Christian—one who is established in the whole circle of truth, in contrast to a babe. Established in the truth we should be united together in one common faith and in the knowledge of the Son of God, the One in whom every truth of the faith is centred. To touch the truth of the Person of the Son of God is to undermine the faith.

The great end set before us is that we all arrive at "a full grown man" according to the measure of the stature of the fulness of Christ. It is not said "full grown men" but "a full grown man", as the saints are viewed corporately as setting forth the fulness of Christ—the One in whom the new man is seen in fulness, or perfection. It may be said that we shall never attain to this perfection down here. This may be so, indeed is so, but God cannot set before us a standard that is less than perfect.

Coming to the unity of the faith, and of the knowledge of the Son of God would preserve us from being tossed to and fro, and carried about by every wind of doctrine. Alas! in Christendom there are many who seek to deceive with fair words, and who act "in unprincipled cunning with a view to systematized error" (N.Tr.). It is generally found that behind every attack on the Person of Christ, whatever form it may take, there is a whole system of error. If we are not established in the true knowledge of the Son of God, we shall surely miss our way, and be led into a system of error. Moreover, it is not enough to hold the truth in the head; if it is to be effective, and preservative, it must be held in love (verse 15, N.Tr.).

Verse 16 brings us to what Christ Himself does directly for the edifying of the body, as the Apostle says, "*From whom* the whole body ... maketh increase". Individuals who exercise gifts pass away, or change, with the passing of time, but Christ remains, and His gracious ministry for the body will go on to the end in spite of all our failure. "Having loved His own which were in the world, He loved them unto the end."

Philadelphia and Laodicea
BIBLE READING ON REVELATION 3:7-22

It is a great mercy that, from the addresses to these two churches, we can learn exactly that which has the Lord's approval in these last days, as well as that which He condemns. Thus, when surrounded by the corruptions of Christendom, we are not left to form our own judgment as to the evil, nor to rest in our own conclusions as to what is suited to the Lord. We have His mind revealed to us.

In addressing these churches the Lord generally assumes a judicial aspect, because there is so much to condemn. In Philadelphia, where there is nothing that the Lord condemns, He presents Himself in a moral way, as, "He that is holy, He that is true", for their encouragement. To the church in Pergamos the Lord presents Himself as, "He which hath the sharp sword with two edges". To the church in Thyatira, He is the One "who hath His eyes like unto a flame of fire". With the sword and fire we naturally connect the thought of judgment. Holiness and truth set forth moral qualities.

Evidently Philadelphia is surrounded by conditions that are the opposite of all that is "holy" and "true". It has often been said that the conditions set forth in the last four churches go on to the end of the church period. The corruptions of Christendom in their most extreme form are seen in the Papal system as represented by Thyatira. The deadness of Protestantism is set forth in Sardis, and the self-sufficiency of Modernism in Laodicea. In the midst of all this corrupt profession the Lord indicates in the address to the church in Philadelphia that, until the end, there will be those that have His approval. It follows that we should have before us that which He approves, and seek to answer to it.

It would surely be presumption for any company of people to claim to be Philadelphians. That such saints exist, and will exist, under the eye of the Lord until the end seems clear. For the Lord's reference to His coming infers that such will be found at His coming. We are safe in saying this is what the Lord approves in the day in which we live: it is for each one to seek to answer to His mind, and to walk with those who are like-minded in having this object before them, and then leave the Lord to say how far we have done so. We do well to remember that it was not the Philadelphians who said of themselves, "We have kept His word and not denied His Name": it was the Lord who said these things of them.

If seeking to answer to His mind ourselves, the Lord would give us the sense that, however poor and insignificant we may be in the eyes of the world, yet we are amongst those who aim at keeping His word and not denying His name. The Lord says to Philadelphia, "Thou hast kept My word." His word was communicated through Paul and other Apostles, as well as through John. All His word must be included.

It is helpful to see that the way in which the Lord presents Himself to the Philadelphians exactly corresponds with His own path through this world. He was "the holy"—"holy, harmless, undefiled, separate from sinners." He was "the true"—the true witness to God before men. And "to Him the porter openeth." In spite of all the opposition He had to meet, and though resisted on every hand, nothing could prevent Him from finding His own sheep. He was the great Shepherd, to Him the door was opened, and not one of His sheep will be lost.

The "key of David" alludes to the prophecy of Isaiah in which Eliakim prefigures Christ as the One to whom the government of the world is committed, and who has the key to all the blessings connected with the house of David (Isaiah 22:20-22). The symbol implies that the one who holds the key, has the power; but it suggests, not exactly power in display against the wicked, which would be connected with the sword, but rather power used on behalf of His poor people. Thus the Lord can say, "I have set *before thee* an open door."

It is striking that while the Lord says of this church, "I know thy works", yet He says nothing about their works. In the addresses to Thyatira, and other churches, in which there is so much to condemn, the Lord also has much to say about their works. Here where there is nothing that He condemns, there is nothing said about the works. This would indicate that they had nothing striking in the way of display before the world, but their works were known to the Lord.

This is in keeping with the Lord's words, "Thou hast a little strength." The Lord, however, does not say, "Thou hast no strength." Of Sardis the Lord has to say "Thou art dead." Obviously a dead man has no strength. Again, of the Laodiceans the Lord says, "Thou art wretched, and miserable, and poor, and blind, and naked." It is clear that such have no strength. But of the Philadelphians the Lord can say, "Thou hast a *little* strength." They had sufficient strength to overcome the corruption, deadness, and self-sufficiency, of the great Christian profession by which they are surrounded. It is noticeable that God's work has always been done in circumstances of weakness. Nothing can be weaker than a little babe; yet the Lord came into the world as such. He had not where to lay His head as He passed through it, and at last He was crucified in weakness.

There are four things said of this assembly which have the Lord's approval:—

"Thou hast a little strength";

Thou "hast kept My Word";

Thou "hast not denied My name";

"Thou hast kept the word of My patience."

If, then, these are the things that the Lord approves, we do well to seek to enter into their meaning, in order to answer to them.

If there are those who seek to keep the Lord's word and not deny His name, they will at once find they are faced with opposition; and the question at once arises, How can those with only a little strength face the opposition? The Lord seems to say "I will see to that, I will set before thee an open door." As we have seen, when the Lord was here He was faced with every kind of opposition, but the door was held open for Him, and now He holds the door open for His poor people, and no one can resist His power.

We are living in a day when on every hand the inspiration of Scripture is being denied, and we have to stand firmly for the great truth that "All Scripture is given by inspiration of God." Nevertheless we may do this and yet fail to keep His word. To keep Christ's word implies that we seek to answer to His mind as revealed in His word. His word implies the whole truth of Christianity whether revealed by the Lord to His disciples when here, or revealed through the Holy Spirit to His apostles after He had gone back to the Father. Alas! there is not a truth of Christianity that is not denied somewhere, by someone, in some form, in Christendom to-day. To keep His word implies that we walk in the light of these truths revealed in His word.

"Thou hast not denied My name." We live in a day when every truth as to the Person of Christ is being denied. Nevertheless, "not denying His Name" implies a great deal more than refusing to deny His Deity and His perfect Manhood. To present forgiveness of sins in any other name is to deny His name. For believers to gather together in any other name is to deny His name. To name His name and remain in association with iniquity is to deny His name.

The fourth characteristic, that has the Lord's approval, is, "Thou hast kept the word of My patience." We have seen that we must not limit the thought of keeping His word, to merely holding to the truth of the inspiration of Scripture; and again, we cannot limit not denying His name to the fact that we do not deny His Deity and Manhood. So with this last word of approval; keeping the word of His patience implies more than waiting for His coming. It indicates, rather, *the spirit* in which we wait.

The Lord Jesus, as He passed through this world, met on every hand with contradiction, opposition, and insults, but in the presence of every false accusation and insult He "held His peace", He "answered never a word." He was not indifferent to the insults but He met them all with infinite patience. So through the centuries His people have been persecuted, sent to the stake, and stoned; they have had to meet insults and reproaches, and the Lord has not publicly interfered. He is not, however, indifferent to the sufferings of His people, but He is waiting in patience until His enemies will be made His footstool. And we are called to wait with Him in patience. So the Apostle can say to the Hebrew believers, in the presence of the spoiling of their goods, "Ye have need of patience ... for yet a little while and He that shall come will come, and will not tarry" (Hebrews 10:36, 37). Again, James can write to believers, in the presence of their sufferings, "Be ye also patient ... for the coming of the Lord draweth nigh" (James 5:8).

The thought of patience then is submission to trials and wrongs, while waiting for the day when all will be dealt with. Again, when Christians are tempted to interfere with the politics of this world they may well remember the patience of Christ. We are left here not to right the wrong of the world but to represent Christ. If someone had suggested to Simeon, in his day, to join a society for the improvement of Jerusalem, would he not have refused with the words, "I am waiting for the consolation of Israel"? He knew, and we know, that One is coming who will right every wrong; with this knowledge we can keep the word of His patience which tells us that He is waiting until all His enemies are put under His feet. So we can say:—

A "little strength" indicates *dependence* on the Lord;

Keeping His word, indicates *obedience*;

Not denying His name, implies *devotedness*; and

Keeping the word of His patience, *endurance*.

When the Lord says, in verse 10, "I also will keep thee out of the hour of temptation, which shall come upon all the world, to try them that dwell upon the earth", He speaks of the judgments that are coming upon professing Christendom that has given up the truth of the heavenly calling and settled down to dwell upon the earth. The Lord assures those saints that from these judgments they will be kept. It is of course true for every believer; but those whose ways have the approval of the Lord have the blessed assurance of His promise in the secret of their souls.

It is important to see that the promises to the different churches are not special and confined to the particular church, and so exclusive of others. In each church the Lord *emphasises* certain favours that would encourage His people in the particular circumstances in which they are found, but which in themselves are to be the portion of all true saints.

While the Lord's word to this church is one of approval and not condemnation, there is a word of warning and encouragement. In the presence of opposition the Lord says, "Behold, I come quickly; hold that fast which thou hast, that no man take thy crown." The Lord has been saying to these saints, *Thou hast* a little strength, *thou hast* kept My word, and *thou hast* not denied My name; now He exhorts them to hold fast that which *thou hast*.

Then the Lord encourages to hold fast by setting before them the glories of the coming day. It will be noticed how often the little word "My" is used in the course of this address. The Lord speaks of "*My* word", "*My* name", "*My* patience", "the temple of *My* God", "the city of *My* God", "and *My* new name". It intimates to us how blessedly the Lord associates these saints with Himself, and His things, both now and in the coming day of glory.

The new name would seem to be a name the Lord takes in connection with the new and heavenly order of things. A name that we cannot know until we are there; now we only know in part. Of that coming day we read, "They shall see His face, and His name shall be in their foreheads." We shall see Him, and He will be seen in us. At last we shall come out in His likeness and truly represent Him. Though there is nothing that the Lord condemns in this church, He speaks of overcoming since there was the danger of giving up. We are to overcome the tendency to let go things that the Lord approves.

We have already noticed that the Lord presents Himself in a moral way to the Philadelphians by way of *encouragement*. To the Laodiceans He presents Himself morally, but in the way of *rebuke*. As the Amen the Lord is the confirmation and fulfilment of all the promises of God (2 Corinthians 1:20). He was ever "faithful" to God and "the true witness" before the world. And in Him we see the beginning of an entirely new Creation. These things should have been set forth in the Church. We should have confirmed the calling of God by living as a heavenly people. We should have been faithful to God and a witness before the world. Moreover the saints should have been "a kind of firstfruits of His creatures" by setting forth the character of those who will be in the new creation (James 1:18).

Nevertheless, though the church has broken down in responsibility, every thought of God is fulfilled in Christ. It still remains true that He is "the Amen". He closed His perfect life with the words, "It is enough"; He completed His work on the Cross with the words, "It is finished"; and He completes His millennial reign with the words, "It is done" (Luke 22:38; John 19:30; Revelation 21:6). In Isaiah 65:16, God is twice spoken of as the "God of truth". This word, in the twenty other occasions of its use is rightly translated "Amen". God is the God of Amen—the God who brings everything to completion.

Laodicea sets forth the last stage of professing Christendom as seen by the Lord. It is a condition of total indifference to Himself. Such a condition is nauseous to Him, and the church will be utterly rejected by Him as a witness for Himself on earth, as He says, "I will spue thee out of My mouth." Then, when the professing church is utterly rejected by Christ as totally unfit for Himself, the Beast will say, as it were, "Now it is altogether fit for me, and I will take it up and carry it" (Revelation 17:3-7).

Having had the Lord's estimate of the Christian profession in its last stage, we are now told what the profession says of itself—"I am rich and increased with goods and have need of nothing." What is this but self-occupation, self-satisfaction, and self-sufficiency? But the Lord exposes to these self-satisfied people their true condition, "Thou art wretched, and miserable, and poor, and blind and naked." Then the Lord makes one last appeal to this great Christless profession. In the most touching way He seems to say, "If you are wretched, and miserable, and poor, and blind, and naked" you are the very ones for Me, and I am the only One for you, I counsel thee to buy of Me the gold that thou mayest be rich; the raiment that thou mayest be clothed, and the eye salve that thou mayest see.

Further we see that in the midst of this great profession that becomes so nauseous to Christ there are individuals that He owns and loves, though their associations may be such as to call for rebuke and chastening. Nevertheless, the hand that smites is moved by a heart that loves. Then we have the Lord's last touching words, "Behold, I stand at the door and knock; if any man hear My voice, and open the door, I will come in to him, and will sup with him, and he with Me"—words that show that, while it is too late to get back to any great public witness, or display before the world, it is not too late to get back to communion with Christ.

It is striking that this is the only address in which the Lord presents Himself as a pattern for the overcomer. He says, "even as I also overcame, and am set down with My Father in His throne." The last words to the disciples were, "In the world ye shall have tribulation, but be of good cheer *I have overcome* the world" (John 16:33). Christ overcame the world of His day—the world of corrupt Judaism that rejected Himself, and He has been exalted to the Father's throne. We are exhorted to overcome the world of our day—corrupt Christendom that has put Christ outside its door. Thus overcoming we shall find ourselves in reproach and obscurity in this present world; but in the world to come we shall have the appreciation of Christ by being made the sharers of His throne.

The Head of the Church

Scriptures read:
Ephesians 5:22-23; 4:14-16; 1:22-23;
Colossians 1:15-19; 2:8-10, 18-19

"Christ is the Head of the Church." I have again read this expression from Ephesians 5 because I have a real desire that this great fact should take fresh hold upon our hearts. Just for a moment I want to turn your thoughts back over the history of the Church, for I think I can show you from Scripture that it was losing sight of Him that has been the root of all failure.

I take you first to 1 Corinthians because I want you to think of the state of things that marked that Assembly. We think we are in days of great weakness; we are, but I have yet to see greater weakness than that which marked that Assembly. They were weak spiritually, they were unable to deal with moral evil—evil of such a character that it would not have been tolerated among the heathen. Then, they had sunk to such a state that they had turned the Lord's Supper into a common meal, and there were those there who were getting drunk.

I hear people say that the cause of weakness to-day is the lack of gift, but the Assembly at Corinth had every gift. We are told so, and yet gift did not hold them.

I want that simple fact to stand out before you. Do not say that lack of gift is the cause of spiritual weakness; it is not. Then another thing I want to call your attention to in connection with it, is this—in spite of great weakness and failure there was, thank God, recovery. However great the weakness may be, there is ever a way of recovery.

Let me turn next to that remarkable sketch of Church history that we get in Revelation 2 and 3. When He addresses the Church at Ephesus with so much He could commend, He has to call attention to the beginning of all the trouble. "Thou hast left thy first love." He had lost the place that belongs to Him. As you go down the prophetic history of the Church in those chapters, you come to that which speaks of recovery, and in connection with that I want to speak of our own position. I want you to think of the way in which the Lord in His great goodness brought about recovery.

After the darkness of centuries there came long ago the presentation of the Gospel in all its grandeur. Then another work commenced, in this and other lands; the work of the Spirit of God awakening in the hearts of a few of His saints a sense of what was due to the Lord. They saw Him as Head of the Church, and found themselves unable to go on in the associations in which they were.

What did He do? He raised up gifts, to instruct those who in affection of heart answered His claims, to instruct them regarding His Church. That is why I desire to speak to you these few minutes not of the Church but of Him.

Let me turn back a minute to Ephesians 5, because there you get brought before us the claims He has upon us by reason of His affection. He has expressed His love for us in a way that puts it beyond all controversy. He loved the Church and He gave Himself for it. He is still occupied with our welfare, it is a concern of His heart. What answer are we going to give to Him?

As we read in chapter 4, He has provided everything in connection with our need. He has made adequate provision for the need of His Church and you can depend upon it that these resources are as true and as available today, as they were on the first day of the Church's history. He has not changed one solitary bit.

Now come just for a moment to the Colossians. You get the Spirit of God unfolding before your vision the greatness and glories of Christ so that we may know the resources that are His.

We hear His voice speaking to us of what He could do for His people. How He delights to open out before our vision the treasures of wisdom and knowledge, and to bring to our hearts all the great things that He has secured by His death. The object of His affections is the Church. He is occupied with it. We forget Him, He never forgets us. He would recall our hearts to Himself and He would say to us, "Let Me show you what I can be to you."

There is not a single reason why you should not enjoy everything that the Church enjoyed in the days of her brightest history. It is not a question of natural wisdom, or ability. It is a question of Him having His place. He delights to take hold of the most unlikely material and to show how, by His power, He can bring to the hearts of His people the knowledge and enjoyment of the things that are in His heart. There are two things that we need.

We need wisdom, we need power; where are we going to get them? They are both in Christ alone. There is no resource that God has outside Him. He is God's wisdom and God's power, so surely He is sufficient for us. All His thoughts for His own, though clearly stated in the Scriptures, had lain dormant for centuries, but He made them living realities to His people. We will not speak of ourselves, but we can speak of those to whom His word, and the glory that belongs to Him, was everything. They were prepared to give up everything for Him.

Do not tell me that a hundred years has made any difference, that what He did a hundred years ago He cannot do to-day: I know Him too well; I know He can.

During the last few years we have seen great efforts made to bring together various sections of the Church of God and I looked in vain for any reference to what was due to *His Name* in connection with it. Do not let it be so with us, my friends, let it be that His Name is *everything to us*. It will make a difference; of course it will!

In closing, there is a remarkable expression that I want to leave with you. "YE are complete in Him." We need not go outside Him. We need no one but Himself. We are complete in Him. Let us seek grace to give Him His place—shall I say, upon our knees? I think I may. We walk from Him with our head up. The way back to His presence is on our knees, of that there is no question.

Let us seek that He may have His place in connection with His Church. Ephesians 5:33, says, "Let … the wife see that she reverence her husband." Let us see that we rightly reverence our great exalted Head. May God grant us the grace to do it.

Antecedents to Assembling together

SCRIPTURE READ: HEBREWS 10:12-25

From the above scriptures we see that there are obviously antecedents or preliminary conditions which are essential to our coming together in assembly on a real basis.

First, the forgiveness of sins is the indispensable initial requirement. In Hebrews 8 where the terms of the New Covenant are specified, this matter is stated last. But so far as the individual is concerned it must be entered first. No one is entitled to be reckoned a Christian, in the real sense of the word, who has not his or her sins forgiven.

Their sins and iniquities will be remembered no more. Only God could do that. No lesser person could blot out the memory of sins. Christ offered one sacrifice for sins and sat down for ever, even as by that one offering He has perfected the sanctified for ever, (or in perpetuity, i.e., without break or cessation for a moment). All this is in contrast to the previous dispensation of law, wherein the priests daily offered the same sacrifices which were unavailing for the removal of sins, while they indicated that in God's good time He would Himself provide the Sacrifice of infinite value.

Second, the witness of the Spirit (in verse 15) presupposes the Spirit having been given to the believer. The Spirit gives testimony to the efficacy and the peerless value of the work of Christ. The prophetic passages in the Old Testament were ever recurrent as to His coming and His work. The Spirit's witness in the heart of the believer is consonant with the witness of the Scriptures. There are well-meaning Christians (who ought to know better) who aver that the Scriptures are not important as they merely confirm what has been already established in their hearts by the Spirit. However plausible that may seem to be, it conceals a subtle error. The statement arises from defective teaching, because it is exactly the opposite way round. The Spirit confirms in our heart what is set forth in the Scriptures.

There are two great spiritual agencies at work: viz., the Spirit of Truth and the spirit of error. The Apostle John in his Epistle shows that there are two infallible discriminating tests to which every spirit may be subjected. The spirits which are in accord with the Spirit of Truth (a) confess Jesus Christ come in flesh, i.e., the true import of His incarnation: (b) they hear the Apostles, i.e., they listen to the messages conveyed in the Epistles as real messages from God through the Apostles.

It is fashionable in religious circles nowadays to speak in a disparaging way about Paul's opinion or John's opinion as though, if either were living to-day, he would have expressed himself otherwise than he did in the first century. If the Scriptures are valued as the living Word it is impossible to entertain the thought that the passage of time will alter the statement of the One who knows no variableness nor shadow of turning. If we do not pay attention to the Scriptures then our minds become the playground of evil spirits, which will speedily lead us to adopt the ideas of the spirit of error. With such considerations in view we may well exclaim:

> *O to grace how great a debtor*
> *Daily I'm constrained to be!*

But the Spirit is a real entity. He constantly bears testimony to the unchanging efficacy of the work of Christ. Thus the consciousness of forgiveness of sins is established in the believer's heart. We have the Spirit who knows every element of the value of Christ's work. Our having the Spirit introduces the thought that we are the subjects of the Spirit's teaching.

Third, we are apt to be occupied solely with oral teaching. Again referring to Hebrews 8 we see that the second feature of the New Covenant, to be established with the House of Israel in the day to come, is that it will be unnecessary for anyone to teach his neighbour (i.e. orally); for all will know the Lord from the least (i.e. the little ones) to the greatest (i.e. the grown-up person). But the blessings of the New Covenant are now known by the Christian through the Spirit's residence in him.

God has given us His Spirit that we may be conscious that His love has removed in the death of His Son everything that was between Himself and us. To know God there must be no distance between. In the far country, whatever the prodigal might have heard of his father's love, he could never have been deeply conscious of it there. To know God by being near Him is very different from believing a report about Him. The result is that we not only believe the report but we love the One of whom the reports speaks. The Lord Jesus has been given as the Covenant that God's disposition towards men might be known (Isaiah 49:8). Then the love of God being poured forth into our hearts leads us to love one another. "Ye are taught of God to love one another" (1 Thessalonians 4:9). No orthodox formality and ecclesiastical rectitude can ever make up for the lack of love. No matter what argument may be advanced to substantiate the claim of being well taught, it cannot be of value, if love to the saints is not being manifested.

Fourth, we have boldness (i.e. liberty or confidence) to enter the Holiest by the blood of Jesus — the new and living way which He has consecrated for us through the veil, that is His flesh (verses 19, 20). God has opened the way to us unreservedly that we may enter where He is adored, and where we can survey without a veil the glory and majesty of His ways in Christ. In the past dispensation only the High Priest could enter there, once a year, not on account of his own merit but only in a representative way, carrying the blood to sprinkle on the mercy-seat, typifying the perfect offering of Christ.

Everything in the Holiest is in accord with the love of God. Christ is the Ark of the Covenant and the Mercy-seat. Every thought of God for the blessing of man is secured in Christ as the Ark of the Covenant, as He is also the propitiation or Mercy-seat where God can meet man in all his need. What streams of praise would mark our gathering together if we apprehended the privilege of approach in order to view Christ in the Holiest!

God's coming out in the revelation of Himself through the death of the Lord Jesus becomes our way of going in. As a new way it is a spiritual process which supersedes all the process of man on probation and shows his total rejection by God. The way is ever fresh and living because God is revealed in love. In the holiest we apprehend what His mind is.

In the day of glory to come, Israel under the New Covenant will have the forgiveness of sins, the Spirit poured out on them like a deluge and they will be taught of God, but they will never enter the Holiest, nor have intelligence of God's ways nor apprehend His glory, as the saints of this dispensation have the privilege to do. In the process we have wonderful support because we have the Great Priest over the House of God. He is the same unchangeable Person whose eye never slumbers, nor do His hands hang down for a moment of time.

The thrice repeated expression "Let us" shows that the practical bearing of this process implies conditions or responsibility. A "true heart" means that the heart responds to the love of God. "The full assurance of faith" implies that the privilege is not thought to be beyond our apprehension. "Our hearts sprinkled from an evil conscience" indicates that the offering of Christ is known in such a way that our hearts do not condemn us. "Our bodies washed with pure water" would require that our conduct and associations are consistent with the fact that Christ received from the world only a cross and a grave!

We shall then be holding fast the confession of our hope without wavering. We shall continue steadfastly maintaining a resolute front to the enemy as the Christians did at first—because God is not slack concerning His promise. He is faithful! Whatever He has said He will perform in His own good time.

In the long run (because the Christian's pathway is not a short race as a rule), we shall be very considerate for each other; stimulating love and good works, being examples to the flock of God. Parallel with this we shall be found assembling ourselves together and encouraging each other thereby, and in an increasing way as we see the Day of

ANTECEDENTS TO ASSEMBLING TOGETHER

Glory approaching. We must be confirmed in the sense of the imminence of that event, without making any claim to having particular insight to the future. However, everything points to the conclusion of man's day of glory as coming to a sudden end. Man's ingenuity and success in the triumph of mind over matter is getting to such a pitch that he cannot brook denial in his search after the essential nature of things. This was expressed long ago by Sir William Hamilton very aptly:

> *"On earth there is nothing great but man,*
> *In man there is nothing great but mind."*

But man seems bent on using his great powers to encompass the death of his fellows. God must speedily intervene to end the chaos and the welter of blood in human affairs, in order that He, whose right it is to reign, shall reign to the Glory of God and the everlasting benefit of a redeemed creation.

Our Wealth—Our Walk
Scriptures read:
Ephesians 1:3; 2:8-10; 3:8-10; 4:1-2; 5:18-21; 6:10-13

I desire, as the Lord may enable me, to give a brief survey of this priceless portion of His holy Word. I shall summarise by saying that we have:

In chapter one, *God's Will*; In chapter two, *God's Work*; In chapter three, *God's Wisdom*; In chapter four, *The Believer's Walk*; In chapter five, *The Believer's Witness*; In chapter six, *The Believer's Warfare*. Let us go over them briefly.

First, God's Will. I wonder my dear fellow-believer, if you realize that your name is in God's Will. If a wealthy friend were to die and you knew your name was in his will, I suppose the first thing you would do would be to see how much was against your name: in the second place, to put in a claim for it; and in the third place, having got it, to live in the enjoyment of it.

Do you know your name is in God's will? It was written there before the foundation of the world. How much is against your name? Chapter 1 verse 3 supplies the answer

"Every spiritual blessing". We could not have anything greater or more wonderful than that which God has willed for us. All the wealth of God is for the possession and enjoyment of every true believer in the Lord Jesus Christ.

It is absolutely sure, because it is in heavenly places, which means, by the way, that as all the blessings which God has been pleased to give us are heavenly, then we are not an earthly but a heavenly people. These blessings are in Christ, therefore they are absolutely sure.

Most of us, perhaps all of us, have read verse three in Ephesians 1 times without number, we are familiar with it; some of us have known it practically all our life, but to what extent have we taken it home to ourselves, so as to enter into the enjoyment of all the wealth of blessing that is ours in Christ? Let me emphasize once more, we are blessed with "every spiritual blessing". We could not have anything more comprehensive than that. Everything that the heart of God could conceive for us is ours, and He has willed His best for those who are so dear to His heart.

We realize the greatness of our blessing as we realize the *source* of it—we shall speak of the *cost* of it later. As we realize it, what can we do but bow in the presence of our God, and in the language of this verse say with the Apostle "Blessed be the God and Father of our Lord Jesus Christ".

If I may go back to my illustration—the wealthy person might will some of his wealth to some favourite friend, but, after he had done so, there might be something in the conduct of the friend that would cause the person to change his will and blot his name out. What has happened in our case? God had written our name in His will before the foundation of the world. We come down to the region of time, sin came in, and you and I were born in sin. Did that alter God's disposition toward us? Not in the slightest. Why did He put our name in His will before the foundation of the world? Because He loved us.

In verses four and five of chapter 2 we read of "God's great love wherewith He loved us, even when we were dead in sins." Could you imagine anything more loathsome, anything more unlovely, than a person "dead in sins"? That is your condition and mine by nature. Even when we were dead in sins, God loved us with what the Spirit of God calls His great love.

It was great because God, before His will could be carried out, must spare from His side the Beloved of His heart, for "God so loved the world that He gave His only begotten Son, that whosoever believeth in Him should not perish, but have everlasting life." Such was His love for us, when we were dead in sins, that Christ died to effect atonement, that redemption might be accomplished, that God's purpose might be fulfilled, and that you and I might be in His presence, as sons before His face. Therefore God has wrought the most wonderful transformation. We, who were dead in sins, have been quickened with Christ, raised up and made to sit in heavenly places in Christ Jesus. Later in chapter 2, we find that we have been formed into a wonderful organism spoken of as "one body". Why has God done all that?

First, for His own pleasure, for the glory of His name, for the delight and satisfaction of His heart, that in the coming ages He might display His workmanship to a wondering universe, and in that show the surpassing riches of His grace in His kindness toward us through Christ Jesus.

Everything is from God; everything is for God; everything goes back to God in that worship that delights His heart. How wonderful indeed is God's work!

In chapter 3 we see the wisdom of God. There is such a tendency with a lot of people to-day to be satisfied with the knowledge of sins forgiven, and an assured hope of Heaven when they die. But when we read this Epistle to the Ephesians we learn that this would not satisfy the heart of God. He has purposed much more than that. As we proceed to chapter 3 we go from one thing to another, until we are lost in the wondering contemplation of it. The Apostle points out how all believers form this wonderful organism of which he speaks as "one body".

There is something that has been set up in this world, such as never existed before, and that will not be seen in the same way again: the Church — the body of Christ— to represent Christ, to show forth the beautiful features of Christ, to be the expression in this world of what Christ was, when He was in the world, and to be here for the pleasure and glory of God.

Heavenly intelligences find in the Church an object lesson as they look down, and learn the manifold wisdom of God. In this hall to-night are found people from different places, men and women of different temperaments, living different lives, and under different conditions, yet part of that one body under one Head, with one blessed witness, one Object, one heart, and of one mind as to the greatness of our Lord Jesus Christ. No one could accomplish that but God, but that is exactly what God has accomplished, and I have no hesitation in saying that as the Heavenly Intelligences look down tonight they can still see in the church the manifold wisdom of God.

Chapter 4 is practical. Our responsibility comes in there. If God has come out to us in all the richness of His grace, He looks to us for response. In chapters 1, 2 and 3 we have Divine purpose and there our responsibility cannot enter. In chapters 4 and 5 we have our privilege and responsibility to walk worthy of the vocation wherewith we are called.

You will find the word *walk* has a very prominent place in chapters 4 and 5. We are to walk worthy of the vocation, to walk in love, to walk as children of light. What we want to-day in Christianity is *walk* not *talk*. The measure of our walk in accordance with the truth is the measure in which we have that truth in power in our souls. Our mental acquaintance may be greater, we may be able to expound it, but we have not got one whit more in power in our souls than that which is expressed in our walk.

I want to take it home to myself, and to say to you as well, that one great cause of the weakness amongst the people of God is that there has been high talk and low walk. We have been able, to a certain extent, to set forth the most wonderful things, but there has been the walk that has not been consistent with the talk, and it has brought reproach on the name of Christ, and has damaged the testimony. We are to walk worthy of the vocation wherewith we are called, with lowliness and meekness, forbearing one another in love. We are set here to be what Christ was when He was here, and He was meek and lowly in heart.

In chapter 5 we have witness. Verse 18 is important. I wonder sometimes if we attach sufficient importance to it. Every believer is indwelt by the Spirit or he would not be a believer, but every believer is not filled with the Spirit, or we should not have this exhortation.

A person filled with the Spirit is not a person who gets into a state of excitement, who becomes very noisy, talking about himself and his wonderful experiences. He does not call attention to himself, but to Christ, and the people with whom he comes in contact will *not* say, "What a wonderful man he is", but, "What a wonderful Saviour he has got." The result of being filled with the Spirit is not necessarily something we might consider heroic. But speaking to ourselves, not to other people, in psalms, and hymns and spiritual songs, singing and making melody in our hearts to the Lord.

The work of the Spirit is to occupy us with Christ, and if we are occupied with Christ we shall not be occupied with ourselves, or our brethren, or the failures of other people. We shall be so in line with the will of God that no matter in what circumstances we may find ourselves, be it sorrow or joy, ups or downs, we have a secret source of rejoicing because we are filled with the Spirit.

In chapter 6 we have the believer's warfare. If we are set to go in for these things which are so beautifully put before us, we may be quite certain of one thing, the enemy will put forth every effort in order to prevent it. If we want to be in the enjoyment of these blessings, if we want to bring, as God's workmanship, glory to His Name, the enemy will seek to hinder us. If we want to be here walking worthy of the vocation wherewith we are called, and witnessing for Christ, the enemy will seek to defeat us.

There is nothing God has left out of account, nothing He has not thought of, so that our spiritual prosperity might be furthered. Hence the encouragement of verses 10 and 11.

It is not the enemy coming in the character of "a roaring lion", but rather the wiles of the devil. Unless we are living near the Lord, we shall be caught by these wiles. The protection against that is "the whole armour of God". God provides it, and He gives it to us. The only thing we have to do is to put on, not a bit of it, but "the whole armour of God" that we may be able to withstand in the evil day and having done all to stand.

That armour is for our protection. It has been remarked that there is in the armour no provision for the back. We are not supposed to turn our backs to the enemy but to be "strong in the Lord, and in the power of His might", to show a bold front, and, in the strength of the Lord, to withstand. Then victory will be ours through Christ.

May the Lord bless His word, encourage our hearts, and give us to know a little more of the reality of these things, and then, in the power of them, go on to enjoy them and bless God for them.

Christ, the Pattern of the Christian Life

SCRIPTURE READ: PHILIPPIANS 2:1-16

We know that Paul, who wrote the Epistle to the Ephesians, also wrote the Epistle to the Philippians. There is, however, this difference, in the Epistle to the Ephesians he writes as an Apostle, whereas, in the Epistle to the Philippians he does not speak of himself as an Apostle, but simply as a servant. The reason is plain; in the Epistle to the Ephesians, there are unfolded to us the highest truths of Christianity, which could only be revealed to us through an Apostle. But in the Epistle to the Philippians Paul unfolds to us the experiences of a Christian which are possible for all believers. In Ephesians, then, we have revealed to us the great truths of Christianity; in Philippians we have the experiences of a believer who lives in the light of these truths.

To bring home to us the blessedness of these experiences, the Apostle presents, in a very lovely and attractive way, the Person of Christ; for He is the source and pattern of all true Christian experience. In chapter 1, the Apostle speaks of Christ as his life; he says, "For me to live is Christ." He had no other object in life than Christ. In chapter 2, he looks back and presents Christ in his wonderful path on earth, in order to set before us the pattern of the Christian life expressed in perfection. In chapter 3, the Apostle looks on to Christ in the glory, and he sees that the life leads to the place where Christ is, and that every believer is called on high to be with Christ and like Christ. In chapter 4, the Apostle looks around and sees that while we are here we have to face enemies, and meet sorrows, and trials, and cares, and the question arises, How can we get through such a world? The answer is found in Christ, for, says the Apostle, "I can do all things through Christ which strengtheneth me."

Thus in chapter 1, we have Christ our life; in chapter 2, Christ the pattern of the life; in chapter 3, Christ the object and end of the life; and in chapter 4, Christ our strength, to live the life as we pass through this world.

Confining our thoughts to chapter 2, our hearts are attracted to the Lord Jesus Christ, presented in all His lowly grace as He passed through this changing scene. The circumstances which led to this presentation of Christ were these; the Apostle was in prison, and these Philippian saints had sent help to him through Epaphroditus. In those days this was no small undertaking. It involved a journey of one thousand miles. Paul was delighted with this expression of love and fellowship of the Spirit. Nevertheless, he saw in these Philippian saints that which troubled him, for there was a lack of unity amongst them. Therefore he says, "Fulfil ye my joy, that ye be likeminded, having the same love, being of one accord, of one mind." In the course of the Epistle the Apostle refers again, and again, to this one mind. In chapter 1 he desires that they should "stand fast in one spirit, with one mind striving together for the faith of the gospel" (1:27). In chapter 2, the saints are exhorted to be of "one mind" (2:2). In chapter 3, he writes, "let us mind the same thing" (3:15-16). Finally, in chapter 4, he beseeches two sisters to "be of the same mind in the Lord" (4:2).

Perhaps there is nothing more distressing in our own day than to find that so often companies of God's people are distracted through the lack of having one mind in the Lord. What would the Apostle say to-day if he came into any company of the Lord's people? Have we not to hang our heads in shame, as we realize how often we fail in being "likeminded", in "having the same love", in "being of one accord" and "of one mind"?

The Apostle not only rebukes this lack of unity, but he also discloses to us the root of the trouble. He says, "Let nothing be done through *strife* or *vain glory*." Thus we discover that all discord amongst God's people can be traced to "strife" which is the effort to belittle my brother, and "vain glory" which is the effort to exalt myself. Do we not see these two things exemplified in the disciples of the Lord, in the incident recorded in Mark 10? The Lord was journeying to the cross, and coming to Capernaum, and "being in the house", He asked them, "What was it that ye disputed among yourselves by the way?" Immediately we read, "*They held their peace*: for by the way they had disputed among themselves who should be the greatest." Should we be far wrong in saying that the real root of all strife and division among the people of God is that someone wanted to be great? We, of course, can find other reasons, but is this not the primary cause of all division? It is only a little while and we shall all reach home. And when we are home—"in the house"—will not the Lord call us all together and say to us, "What was it that you disputed amongst yourselves by the way?" And in His presence, like the disciples, we shall all be silent with shame. Alas! We can dispute amongst ourselves *by the way*, in the presence of one another; but, in the presence of the Lord we are silent. The fact that we have so often disputed amongst ourselves, only proves how little we have walked in the presence of the Lord.

Having thus discovered to us the root of all discord, the Apostle goes on to show how we can reach "one mind" through each having the lowly mind. To exemplify this lowliness of mind he brings Christ before us; he says, "Let this mind be in you, which was also in Christ Jesus." Then he gives us a lovely presentation of Christ in His path from the glory to the cross. He shows us the *mind* of Christ in taking this path. He stresses four great truths in reference to His lowly path:

First, He "made Himself of no reputation";

Secondly, He "took upon Him the form of a servant";

Thirdly, He "humbled Himself";

Fourthly, He "became obedient unto death".

Naturally we prefer to act in exactly the opposite way. We like to make a reputation for ourselves. We prefer to be served rather than to serve. We seek to exalt ourselves, and prefer to do our own will rather than obey. But Christ made Himself of no reputation. When His disciples said, "All men seek for Thee", He said, "Let us go into the next towns" (Mark 1:37, 38). When men sought to "take Him by force, to make Him a king", "He departed again into a mountain Himself alone" (John 6:15).

He "took upon Him the form a servant". He could say, "I am among you as he that serveth" (Luke 22:27). Again, we read that He laid aside His garments and took a towel, and girded Himself and washed the soiled feet of His way-worn disciples.

He "humbled Himself". He came into this world as a babe, born in a stable, and cradled in a manger. He worked as a carpenter, and associated with simple Galilean fishermen.

He "became obedient unto death." He ever did the will of His Father. Coming into the world, He said, "Lo, I come to do Thy will O God." Passing through the world, He said, "I do always those things which please Him." Going out of the world, He said, "Not My will, but Thine be done."

This, then, was the mind of Jesus—the lowly mind. And to acquire His mind we must be in His company. In His presence we can neither talk of self or seek to exalt self. In His presence we learn of Him and thus acquire something of His lovely character that sets aside self in order to serve others in love.

Seeing, then, that we are exhorted to have this lowly mind of Christ, we may well challenge ourselves by each one asking the question, "With what kind of mind do I face the every-day life?" With what mind do we attempt to preach and teach, and take up the service of the Lord? Is it with the mind that seeks to make something of self; or, in the lowly mind that ignores self to serve others in love?

Then the Apostle reminds us that there is an answer in glory to the lowly life lived on earth. This, too, is blessedly set forth in Christ, for we read, "Wherefore God also hath highly exalted Him, and given Him a Name which is above every name: that at the name of Jesus every knee should bow." He has, indeed, many great and glorious names. "His name shall be called Wonderful, Counsellor, the Mighty God, the everlasting Father, the Prince of Peace", but to wear the name of Jesus, He had to become obedient unto death, even the death of the cross. When nailed to the cross the mocking crowd said, "Let Him now come down." But had He done so, He would have left the name of Jesus behind Him for ever. He would still have been Wonderful, Counsellor, and the Mighty God, but nevermore could He have borne the Name of Jesus. He had to die to make good the Name which is above every Name—the Name of JESUS.

Having exhorted us to have the lowly mind as expressed in Christ Jesus, the Apostle proceeds to set forth the blessed results that would follow. If we could find a company of believers who each set aside self to serve others in love, two things would mark them: —

> First, they would be a company of people in this world for the "good pleasure of God". Thus, the Apostle, exhorting these saints to obey his word as to the lowly mind, goes on to say of such, "It is God which worketh in you both to will and to do of His *good pleasure*" (2:13).
>
> Secondly, being for the good pleasure of God, they would be a company that would be a testimony to unbelievers, as the Apostle can say, "Among whom ye shine as lights in the world" (2:15).

Being for the pleasure of God, and shining as lights in the world implies that they set forth the character of Jesus. For what are the exhortations that follow but a lovely picture of Christ? He did "all things without murmurings and reasonings". As He walked through this world He met on every hand with reproaches and insults; but no murmur ever escaped His lips, and no reasonings as to why such things should be allowed. Men rewarded Him evil for good, and hatred for His love, but He did them no harm. He was blameless and harmless, without rebuke, the light in a dark place, and ever holding forth the word of life in a world of death.

Having then the lowly mind it would become easy in our measure to wear the character of Christ, and thus be here according to the mind of God that we should represent Christ, and thus be a testimony to the world. It may be said that the Church has so completely broken down its responsibility to represent Christ, that it is too late to talk of any public testimony. It may, indeed, be too late to get back to a united testimony to Christ, and too late to get back to a Pentecostal display of power, but it is never too late to get back to Jesus. If we could get back a little more into His company should we not acquire something more of His character, that forgets self to serve others in love? So doing should we not in our little measure still be a testimony to Christ? In His company we cannot think or talk of self, but, like Mary of old, we can hear His word and worship and adore.

The story is told that Charles Lamb and a gathering of his literary friends fell to discussing what they would do if certain great persons came into their midst. The question was asked, "What would they do if Shakespeare entered the room?" Some one replied, "They would all stand up." Then it was asked, "What would happen if Jesus Christ came into their midst?" In answer, Charles Lamb stuttered out, "We should all fall down."

We may recall that great scene described in the fifth chapter of Revelation, which looks on to the time when all the redeemed will be gathered home, and when all the vast host of heaven will join in saying, "Blessing and honour and glory, and power, be unto Him that sitteth upon the throne, and unto the Lamb for ever and ever." Then mark, how does the great scene close? We read, "The four and

"THE EPISTLE OF CHRIST"

twenty elders *fell down and worshipped Him* that liveth for ever and ever." When at last we find ourselves actually in His presence all our self-importance will be withered up for ever, and we shall fall down and worship HIM. Well, indeed, if even now we get into His presence to learn something of the unsearchable riches of Christ, and fall down and worship HIM.

> *We adore Him, and are waiting*
> *To behold Him face to face—*
> *In His presence praise the glory,*
> *Learn the riches of His grace.*

Riches from God's Treasury

SCRIPTURES READ:
ROMANS 2:4; 9:23; 11:33;
EPHESIANS 1:7, 18; 2:4-7; 3:8, 16;
PHILIPPIANS 4:19; COLOSSIANS 1:27; 2:1-3

We have already heard of the wonderful treasures revealed to us and recovered for us, so I thought we might look at some of the great riches that God has in His treasury.

In Revelation 3, where the poor Laodiceans were boasting of their acquired riches, the Lord Jesus counselled them to buy from Him gold tried in the fire to be truly rich. To the Philadelphians He presented Himself as the Holy and the True who had the key of David, and had set before them an opened door which no one could shut. This alludes to Isaiah 22 where Eliakim typified Christ, who is the true Treasurer, and the Nail in the sure place, upon whom all the treasures would be hung. The Lord Jesus, having the key of David, has opened a door for us into the treasury of God.

In Romans 2 we learn how we have been enriched as sinners from *God's riches of goodness, forbearance and longsuffering*. In wondrous goodness God gave His Son to die for us, and led us to repentance, bearing with our stubborness and rebellion, and suffering long our foolishness and waywardness.

Angels have not been chosen to display *the riches of God's glory*, of which Roman 9 speaks, but men who once were sinners, all vessels of mercy. God in sovereign mercy has taken us up and prepared us for glory. Another aspect of this is found in Revelation 21 where the church as the Bride the Lamb's wife, the holy city Jerusalem, comes down from God out of heaven, having the glory of God. Then in Ephesians 3:21, God's glory is seen in the church in Christ Jesus for the age of ages. This church is composed of those who once were Jews and Gentiles, alike vessels of mercy, and unitedly they form a glorious vessel in new creation, God's own workmanship, suitable for the display of His own glory.

Having contemplated God's ways with Israel and considered the judgments of God, Paul exclaims "*O the depth of the riches both of the wisdom and knowledge of God.* How unsearchable are His judgments and untraceable His ways!" There must of necessity lie in the ways and judgments of God that which is beyond the compass of the human mind. Yet if we seek to learn in communion with God His dealing with men, with His people of old, with the nations, and with ourselves, we shall adore, and be enriched with divine wisdom and knowledge from God's treasury.

The riches of God's grace in Ephesians 1 are connected on the one hand with the forgiveness of sins and on the other with the purpose of God. From the same heavenly treasury has come the grace that forgives our sins, and the grace that unfolds to us the mystery of God's will, wherein lies for our apprehension and enrichment divine wisdom and intelligence. Is it not wonderful that God's grace can unfold to sinners, whom He has forgiven, the secret of His will concerning Christ His Beloved in relation to the administration of the world to come.

At the close of chapter 1 we find *the riches of the glory of God's inheritance in the saints.* God is going to possess His inheritance in those He has set apart in Christ, even as He possessed Canaan in Israel, and shall yet possess the earth in the Princes of Israel (Psalm 45:16). Some inheritances are glorious but not rich, others are rich but not glorious, but God's inheritance like Israel's in Canaan—only, infinitely surpassing it—is both rich and glorious. In Deuteronomy 1:7, God describes the glory of Israel's inheritance, and in chapter 8:7-9, we have the description of its riches. Surely this description of the material wealth of the earthly inheritance has its spiritual answer in what God has given to us.

From chapter 2 we learn that in *the riches of God's mercy* He has quickened us out of the moral death in which we were naturally into His own life, and has raised us up and seated us (Jew and Gentile together) in Christ in the heavenly places. In this exalted place God is going to display in us for eternity *the exceeding riches of His grace* in His kindness towards us in Christ Jesus. Even as Mephibosheth, sitting at David's table as one of the king's sons, was a perpetual witness of God's kindness so shall we (who once were rebel sinners) be the eternal witnesses of God's kindness as we sit with Christ in heavenly glory for the coming ages. The erstwhile ravaging Benjamite, Saul of Tarsus, shall be there, and we shall be there, all to display something of the exceeding riches of God's grace.

In the third chapter of Ephesians we read of *the unsearchable riches of Christ*—not the searchable riches of Israel's earthly Messiah, but the unsearchable riches of the heavenly Christ. These unsearchable riches unfold the heavenly glories of Christ, and show the infinite resources at His disposal in relation to every place and office that He fills for the accomplishment of the will of God.

Paul prays in this chapter that the saints might be strengthened according to *the riches of the Father's glory*. This glory shining in the Son surely tells of the deep delight of the Father in the Son, and of His affection for Him. Once the Son was here revealing the grace of the Father, and soon He shall be displayed in the glory of the Father, but meanwhile it is our privilege to be occupied with Him in that glory; and, thus engaged, to be fitted by the Spirit in the inner man to apprehend something of the sphere He fills, and to know the knowledge-surpassing love of Him who fills it.

Is it not comforting to know that the divine treasury is available even for our needs? Nor is it from God's earthly treasury alone that our needs are met. His earthly treasury has the cattle of a thousand hills; the fatness of the earth; and the abundance of the seas. But it is not of this earthly treasury Paul speaks in Philippians 4, but of *God's riches in glory in Christ Jesus*.

As minister of the church the apostle tells the Colossian saints that God desired them to know *the riches of the glory of this mystery*. The mystery was not revealed until the Spirit of God came down from the ascended Christ. It discloses that Christ is the Head of the body the assembly, and that He is the life and resource of the Gentiles who are united to Him. Although rejected by Israel as Messiah, Christ shall yet be among His earthly people with His glory radiating from Jerusalem, but the mystery reveals a heavenly Christ now among the Gentiles, and the prospect of their being glorified with Him in heaven.

The book of God being completed, there is presented for us in Christ the full knowledge of the mystery of God. God is fully known in Him who is the image of the invisible God: so that as we read the word we can have *the riches of the full assurance of understanding* in the mystery of God. In the Son we can learn what God is in the holiness of His nature, in the activities of His grace, and in the life which has been made ours as united to Christ our Head. In this glorious mystery there are hid *all the treasures of wisdom and knowledge*. All that can be known of God lies in it. Philosophy with its appeal to the natural mind boasts of its mysteries, but *every treasure* of wisdom and knowledge lies hidden for our exploration in the mystery of God.

Servants of God who have preceded us have directed us to the wonderful riches of God. Let those of us who are younger seek more and more to explore and acquire the riches available for us in the divine treasury. As we do so we shall be moved to adoration and worship.

"His Fulness"

SCRIPTURES READ:
JOHN 1:14-16; EPHESIANS 1:20-21;
COLOSSIANS 1:16-19; 2:8-10; REVELATION 22:13-16

As the previous speaker was bringing before us the wonderful riches of God's treasury, that are available for us in the Lord Jesus Christ, I felt impressed to say a little as to the Divine fulness that is in the Son of God, as indicated in the scriptures I have just read.

Last night we were hearing from Philippians 2, of the marvellous stoop of the Lord Jesus from the form of God to the form of a Servant. Wonderful and true as that surely was, (our hearts were delighted as we listened), we must ever remember that personally He was no less great when in the Servant's form down here than when subsisting in the form of God. In these scriptures we have read of that Divine fulness, which was in Him in this world, which is still in Him in resurrection, and which will yet come into display in the vessel which is even now being formed, and which will be fitted to display the fulness of Him which filleth all in all.

To begin with then, in John 1 we read how "the Word became flesh ... full of grace and truth"; and again that "of

His fulness have all we received, and grace for grace", or "grace upon grace". It does not say, truth upon truth, for truth has come in a complete and absolute way in the Son. But grace, Divine favour, flows on, ministered to us as needed.

We can trace it a little through this Gospel, chapter after chapter, as meeting varieties of human need. In chapter 2 we see grace manifested at the marriage feast. In chapter 3 as dealing with Nicodemus. In chapter 4 meeting the woman at the well. In chapter 5 with the man at the pool. In chapter 6 feeding the crowds. In chapter 8 with the woman in the temple. In chapter 9 opening the eyes of the blind man. In chapter 11 raising Lazarus, and dealing with his sisters. Grouping them all together, we can indeed say, "Of His fulness have all we received, and grace upon grace."

If we turn now to Colossians 1, we find the Fulness spoken of in a very distinctive way. In the Son *all* fulness was pleased to dwell. Here it seems to be for the reconciliation of all things in the heavens and on earth for the pleasure of the Godhead. While in Genesis 1 we read that God was active in creation, we learn here that it was through the Son that all things were brought into being. In verse 16 there are three prepositions; *"by"* (or "in"), *"by"* and *"for"*. The first indicates the Source; the second, the instrumental Power; the third, the End in view. All three are used in connection with the Son, and are true of Him.

In verse 16 we have, "all things were created by Him", and in verse 20, "by Him to reconcile all things unto Himself". "By" is the same word in both cases, and putting them together, we have this: The Son was instrumental in the creation of all things, and becoming Man He is instrumental through His death in reconciling all things for the pleasure of the Godhead. Then in regard to the "for", He will yet fill all things, as Ephesians 1 states.

In Colossians 2 we read that the Fulness is still dwelling in Him bodily. In Him down here to reconcile all things for the pleasure of the Godhead, it abides in Him in glory, for the support of the members of His Body, in order that they may display now in testimony the virtues of the Head. The word "complete", in verse 10, is connected with the word "fulness" in verse 9, since it means "filled full". The fulness of the Godhead is in Him, and we are filled full in Him. There is every resource that we need in Him now, to enable us to come out for His pleasure in this world. Hence from the Head, "all the body by joints and bands having nourishment ministered, and knit together, increaseth with the increase of God."

In Ephesians 1 our thoughts are carried on to the world to come. In that day Christ will fill all things with His fulness. The vessel will be adequate, fruit of God's own work, to display His fulness to the bounds of the universe. In Colossians that fulness is to be displayed in testimony *now*; in Ephesians to be displayed in glory *in the world to come*. In Ephesians 4 the work of the ministry will go on, "till we all come … unto the measure of the stature of the fulness of Christ."

The verse we read in Revelation 22 came into my mind as I rose. Here again we have the greatness of the Son brought before us. He is the "Alpha and Omega, the Beginning and the End, the First and Last." The three things suggest, Language; Work; Being. He is the embodiment of all that God has to *say*; of all that He *works* for His glory; of all that He *is* in nature and character. The Son abides "the Same".

In verse 16 He presents Himself to us as "I Jesus", the One we heard of from Philippians 2, in His perfect Manhood and His lowly grace. In this last chapter of the Scriptures we are given to see His eternal greatness, and along with that His infinite grace, that will ever be known to us; for He abides, "Jesus Christ, the Same yesterday, and to-day, and for ever."

A Word on Service

SCRIPTURES READ: GENESIS 24 (VARIOUS VERSES);
2 KINGS 4:31-36; PHILIPPIANS 1:18-19

We were reminded very definitely last night that we are living in an age of grace, the outstanding character of which is that God has "blessed us with all spiritual blessings in the heavenlies in Christ." This, He has done apart from any antecedent worthiness in us and apart from any prospect or promise of consequent good behaviour. Yet let us never forget that "we are His workmanship, created in Christ Jesus unto good works, which God hath before ordained that we should walk in them." Because God has blessed us in pure and sovereign grace, there rests upon every believer the obligation to walk worthy of the Lord unto all pleasing and to *serve Him* with diligence.

It is of service that I wish to speak to-night, and to service of some kind we are all committed. The service may be obscure. We may all be truly described as "publicity-shy brethren", but I trust that there is no uncertainty as to the testimony that we bear to the truth of God.

The passages which I have read may appear not only to be unconnected but to have little bearing upon service, but what I would like to take from them, and God helping me to stress, are these features—The Qualities of the True Servant: The Private Exercises of Soul of the Servant: The Servant's Temptations and The Servant's Safeguards, and I may say that I have in mind particularly, service of a public character.

Before touching upon Genesis 24, let me remind you of its setting. In Genesis 21 we have the story of the birth of Isaac. It is the record of the birth of a son, given by promise, supernaturally born, and in whom were centred blessings not only for Israel but for all the nations of the earth. Then wonder of wonders!—the very God who gave, makes the strange demand, "Take now thy son, thine only son Isaac, whom thou lovest, and get thee into the land of Moriah; and offer him there for a burnt offering upon one of the mountains which I will tell thee of." In Genesis 22, we behold the father, whose love for his son we cannot overestimate and before whose consummate faith in God we feel humiliated, about to offer Isaac on Mount Moriah. We behold him trusting where he cannot understand, and in sublime confidence accounting that should Isaac's life be taken from the earth, God would raise him from the dead, "from whence also", we read in Hebrews 11, "he received him in a figure", or as it might read, "as a type".

The succeeding chapter contains no mention of Isaac. He is, as it were, caught out of sight and then in the chapter which we have read to-night, we find the father, sending his eldest and nameless servant, fit type of the Holy Spirit, to find a bride for the Son.

The interpretation in the light of that Divine grace, manifested in the Person of the Son; His death—probably near the same spot some two thousand years subsequently; His resurrection, and the call of the Church, needs no unfolding.

Abraham himself, old and well-stricken in age, presents a delightful object lesson. Here is a beautiful sunset upon the pathway of faith. "The Lord had blessed Abraham in all things." Conscious of it, and conscientiously faithful to the Divine will, he puts his servant upon oath not to take a wife unto his son, of the daughters of the Canaanites. His insight into the Divine purpose is evident as he declares, "The Lord God of heaven … that sware unto me, saying, Unto thy seed will I give this land; He shall send His angel before thee"; and his assurance of Divine favour is manifested.

The qualities of this model servant can only be touched upon and left to the prayerful consideration of each to develop. There was no doubt about *his commission*. He was called upon to engage in a task, making demands for tact, resourcefulness and wisdom, greater than those possessed by ordinary men. He readily undertook to carry out his Master's desires, though he was perfectly aware of the difficulties. Intelligently anticipating them, he sought his instructions from the Master himself. Accepting the commission and in possession of adequate directions, he was marked by *intelligent obedience*, and he set off with the wealth of his Master at his disposal to provide for a successful issue.

Yet in a task so important he realized that each new step in the business must be taken in the spirit of fidelity to his Master and *prayerful dependence* upon God. His prayer for guidance is a model of simple yet fervent request, while his demeanour towards the damsel is an example of that *courtesy* which should ever characterise the servant of God.

Then we read, "The man wondering at her held his peace, to wit whether the Lord had made his journey prosperous or not." This portrays his *watchfulness* for every indication of the Divine Will; while the *thanksgiving* and *worship* of his heart are manifested in that, "The man bowed down his head, and worshipped the Lord. And he said, Blessed be the Lord God of my master Abraham … I being in the way the Lord led me."

Here is a man to whom the success of his errand meant more than meat. His Master's cause must come first. So *intensely earnest* is he that food being set before him he said, "I will not eat until I have told mine errand." The declaration of the errand was not in any sense the glorification of self but it was the glowing account of the Father's purpose for the Son, that Son's position and greatness, and the bride's prospects. "And they rose up in the morning and he said, Send me away unto my master." Such persuasive earnestness does the servant employ that we are not surprised as we hear Rebekah say, "I will go."

May God grant to all of us who seek to win souls for Christ the qualities of this faithful servant!

In what we have been considering there has been all the glamour of a great romance. And, of course, there is nothing more delightful than leading a soul to Christ. But this is one aspect only of the work of the true servant. The more public nature of the work, journeying, appealing, succeeding, may prove a strong attraction to some who are not prepared for the private and agonizing exercises of a servant of God.

We are all, I take it, familiar with the story of the Shunammite called in Scripture "a great woman". Her services to the prophet Elisha were rewarded by the gift of a son, who when grown went out to his father at time of harvest to help with the reaping. Then comes the story of his sudden illness, and his unexpected death. Thereupon with all haste the Shunammite drove to the prophet of God and refused to return without the assurances of his presence and ministry.

The part of the story in which we are now particularly interested is that which deals with the service of Gehazi and the labours of Elisha. "Gehazi passed on before them, and laid the staff upon the face of the child; but there was neither voice nor hearing. Wherefore he went again to meet him, and told him, saying, The child is not awaked." It all appeared most proper and correct. The prophet's staff had doubtless been effectual on occasions, but it was impotent in the presence of death. Gehazi, I imagine, would not have marvelled greatly if the child had awaked, for in all probability he failed to appreciate that the child was dead.

How many there are who although professed servants of God, have no adequate appreciation of the condition of those whose blessing they seek! The gospel of God is not merely a beneficial influence for the recovery of the sick. When received into the soul it is nothing less than life from the dead. It is God's prerogative to bestow life, and the glorious work of God is not likely to be done by those incapable of comprehending its true nature.

But can we not all confess to having engaged in using the prophet's staff? Is not this the great secret of our failure? We have preached the truth, and laid it upon the face of the child or adult, but we ourselves have not agonized in soul. With Gehazi we have been compelled to say, "The child is not awaked." What then shall we do? Let us confess our folly, forsake such ways and take courage from Elisha. "And when Elisha was come into the house, behold the child was dead and laid upon his bed. And he went up ... and he stretched himself upon the child."

Let us note the earnestness of the prophet as he prayed in secret for the dead child. *Secret prayer* is the first essential for blessing. But prayer must be followed by means, without which prayer would only be hypocrisy. There is on the prophet's part a vivid realization of the child's condition as dead; there is too a sympathetic adaptation to the child's state. No difficulty must be too great, nothing too humiliating for the soul-winner.

The prophet, in seeking the life of a child, places his mouth to the child's mouth; his eyes to the child's eyes; his hand to the child's hands; all of which we might be disposed to describe as *contraction* for the prophet, but the scripture emphasises the fact that he *stretched* himself. Let no one imagine that to see things with a child's eyes, to speak things easily understood by a child is a task for any simpleton. The wisest man will have to stretch himself if he would realize his desires for a child's blessing. Results appeared, for "the flesh of the child waxed warm." But the prophet did not forthwith relax his efforts.

We, as servants, are sometimes so elated at obtaining an interest that we stop short at conviction, instead of pressing on and labouring until conversion is certain. "Then he returned and walked in the house to and fro; and went up and stretched himself upon him: and the child sneezed seven times, and the child opened his eyes." He sneezed! Neither a very articulate nor musical sound we admit, but as it betokened life, what joy it must have brought to the heart of Elisha! If we agonize over souls we shall be quick to catch the first signs of grace and of life—the sneeze, the opened eyes—and thanking God, it will be our desire to see the quickened soul nursed for the Lord.

May God grant to us as true servants, this secret exercise of soul in His presence!

But there are the servant's temptations. Every true servant will experience buffeting and trial. Probably it is true to say that the more prominent the servant, the greater the testing. Who so prominent amongst the servants of the Lord as the Apostle Paul, and who so tried? "In labours more abundant, in stripes above measure." Some of his perils we can readily understand. "In perils by mine own countrymen, in perils by the heathen … in perils among false brethren." From some we might almost have been tempted to believe, the blessed Master, in whose service he toiled, would have exempted him. "In hunger and thirst … in cold and nakedness." But in all these he found the Lord with him and His grace sufficient. And besides those things he carried the care of all the churches—apart from grace, an intolerable load. Aye, and temptations not only from without but from within, so that constantly he had to keep his body under.

How great the temptation to every servant to independence and pride, to strife and vainglory. Out of every temptation the servant needs to be saved. Dear brothers and sisters let me ask you: What you are doing for the servants of the Lord? Do you merely patronize them by your presence and do them the honour of listening to their words? Do you sometimes mete out unkind and unjust criticism? To-night I want to exhort you to prayer for their salvation, in the midst of their peculiar temptations. "For I know", says the apostle, "that this shall turn to my salvation through your prayer and the supply of the Spirit of Jesus Christ."

But on whose prayers was he counting? Were they all robust and mature Christians? Well, I suppose, Lydia would be one and the Philippian jailer another: Euodias and Syntyche would be amongst the number. Lydia converted from Judaism: the jailer snatched as a brand amidst paganism: two sisters even now requiring an exhortation to be of one mind in the Lord,—on the prayers of such does the great Apostle count. He does not even ask for their prayers, but takes them for granted. And shall we be less mindful of the servants of the Lord than they?

But the safeguard is twofold "Your prayer and the supply of the Spirit of Jesus Christ." There must be, of course, the unction of the Holy Spirit without which no ministry can be effective but here it is that spirit of meekness and humility which marked Christ, which as it characterizes us will be our surest safeguard. Of this we were powerfully reminded last night when exhorted in the terms, "Let this mind be in you which was also in Christ Jesus."

To this end may these meetings be blessed of the Lord, for His name's sake.

The Seven Words

SCRIPTURES READ:
LUKE 23:32-34, 39-43; JOHN 19:25-27;
MATTHEW 27:46; JOHN 19:28-30; LUKE 23:46

You will recall the words of the aged Simeon as he took the Child Jesus in his arms; said he, "Behold this Child is set for the fall and rising again of many in Israel ... that the thoughts of many hearts may be revealed." The Cross of Christ is the test, by it are laid bare the thoughts of all hearts; but most of all His own thoughts, His deep feelings were revealed there. We learn what they were by the Seven Words that came from His lips.

I want us to consider the Lord Jesus as He was hanging upon a felon's cross. What a place for the Lord of glory! What a place for the Prince of life! Yet there He was, and for that He had come forth from the Father; for that He had left His throne in the glory, and come into the world. And yet as we view His life among men we might well have expected something different. He went about doing good, He was the Servant of their needs; His heart was ever moved with compassion for their sorrows; He healed them, He blessed their children, He wept for them. Surely universal acclamation, an undisputed throne and the crown of His people's affection were His just due; but instead, He was crowned with thorns, spit upon, buffeted, derided, execrated and nailed to the cross. Behold that multitude shouting and jostling there, a high festival for them is the crucifixion of the Nazarene. They have put Him to the utmost suffering and shame that their hell-inspired hatred could devise, but they are not satisfied; they gather round to mock at His sorrows; they make His weakness their jest. "Himself He cannot save", they cry. "Come down from the cross, and we will believe." Wave after wave of that raging hatred broke over Him, the hearts of men were exposed to their very core in that awful hour; but then it was that He spoke. Above the noise of the tempest His voice rises to His Father in prayer. *"Father,"* He cries, *"forgive them, for they know not what they do."* That was His answer, the triumph of divine love over human hate.

He might have prayed another prayer. He might have asked for twelve legions of angels from His Father, and they would have stood between Him and the hosts of men and devils; but He did not; if He had done, it would have meant damnation for that multitude, and for you and me; and He came to save, not to damn. He looked upon that mass of men and beyond them down all the generations to follow and prayed for forgiveness for them, and because of that prayer, repentance and remission of sins are preached in His Name among all nations.

His first word expressed His will for the world of sinners; in His second, He made known His will for every individual sinner that trusts himself to Him. We know not what it was that first arrested the thief at His side, but the Spirit of God had opened his eyes to see, and his heart to believe, and his mouth to confess. He owned his sinfulness and his just desert, and confessed the truth as to the

Person of the Lord. His eyes pierced the surrounding gloom and saw the glory of the coming Kingdom. "Lord," he said, "remember me when Thou comest into Thy kingdom." He claimed the Lord's exclusive attention, as though he and the Lord alone existed in that hour. Was that presumptuous? Nay, it was faith; faith that was answered at once by the grace of the Lord. *"Verily, I say unto thee, to-day shalt thou be with Me in Paradise."* And what a "thee" he was; a polluted wretch unfit to live on earth. How could he be in Paradise? One thing is certain, if the Lord said, "Thou shalt be with Me in Paradise", He would make him fit. "The blood of Jesus Christ His Son cleanseth from all sin."

On that day no two people on earth loved Him more than His mother and John, and there they stood together by the cross. His sufferings and their love to Him had drawn them there. And Jesus said to Mary, *"Woman, behold thy Son"*, and to John *"Behold thy mother."* That most surely meant, "You love Me, love one another." And that disciple took her to his own home that very day, and there they dwelt together in love and unity. In this third word He has expressed His will for all those who love Him, and should not this move our hearts profoundly? He has said to us, "Love one another, as I have loved you", and in this same Gospel we read that He died to gather together in one the children of God that are scattered abroad. Can we think of the cross and quarrel? Can we treat any of His loved ones with indifference as we stand by His cross? His death is the revelation of His love to every one of them, and shall not we love them also? Those outstretched arms embrace the whole of God's family, and He says to us, "Behold My mother and My brethren!"

"My God, My God, why hast Thou forsaken Me?" What mortal mind can understand that cry, or mortal words

explain it? It is the central cry of the seven, and rightly so, for upon its deep mysterious meaning there depends all the glory of God and our salvation. Why was it? The Lord Himself answers the question. "But Thou art holy" (Psalm 22:3). But was not Jesus holy? Yes, He was as holy in His perfect Manhood as in the Godhead glory; just as holy in His own Person when He hung upon that cross as when He created the angels. Then why was He forsaken? I answer for myself—It was for me. That which we were, He was made. Sin, which is eternally and infinitely abhorrent to God, He became, that God's love might reach us in absolute righteousness. The inflexibility of God's justice and the greatness of His love were revealed when that cry broke forth from the darkness and woe of Calvary. He was forsaken that we might be saved. Oh may we ever be preserved from thinking superficial thoughts of our salvation! I admit the mystery of that cry. No creature mind will ever fathom the depths of it. Father, Son and Holy Ghost alone understand it; but throughout eternity it will be the wonder of our hearts and the theme of our song. Jesus, our Saviour, who knew no sin was made sin for us that we might become the righteousness of God in Him.

For the first time the Lord speaks of His physical sufferings. His strength was dried up like a potsherd, and His tongue clave to His jaws. Then broke forth His cry, *"I thirst."* Did not ten thousand angels answer that cry and gird themselves to serve their suffering Lord and, breaking through the hosts of foes that beset Him, refresh His fevered mouth with better water than that of Bethlehem's spring? No. There was no answer to that cry from heaven. And what of men? Will they relent? They have watched Him in His agony: will compassion wake up within their hearts at last? "They gave Me gall for My meat and in My thirst they gave Me vinegar to drink." No there was no succour from men for Him. Man's answer to the Lord's deepest need was vinegar, the sourest thing that nature can produce. But there was more than physical thirst behind that cry. Why was He there at all? Why should He suffer? Because He thirsted for the love of men. And the challenge comes to every one of us this night. What shall be our answer to His thirst? Shall we pour out to Him the love of our hearts undivided, hearts that have been won by His great love? "The Son of God, who loved me and gave Himself for me." What shall the answer be to that? The world still gives Him vinegar. Oh, Christians, let us hasten to His feet and give Him the rich pure wine of our love!

Now we are emerging into the light. Now we reach the triumph; for from His lips there breaks the triumphant cry, *"It is finished."* Every word as to His suffering fulfilled. He had yet to bow His head in death and His side had to be pierced, but in anticipation of that He could cry, "It is finished." We rest upon a finished work. We have many reasons for perfect peace of heart in regard to our relations with God, and this is not the least of them; the work of redemption has been finished by the Son of God, who only could have undertaken it. He has not failed. We glory in redemption accomplished. God is glorified; the devil is defeated; we are saved.

His first word was "Father." His last word is "Father"; and between the two the darkness and tempest. *"Father into Thy hands I commend My spirit."* It is only in Luke's gospel that this cry is recorded, the Gospel that gives His first recorded words, "Wist ye not that I must be about My Father's business?" That business was finished now, not a jot of it left undone, and in the serenity and calm of that knowledge He commends His spirit to His Father and bows His head in death.

What shall our answer be to love so amazing, so divine? What but to yield ourselves up to Him, and, constrained by that love, live henceforth not unto ourselves but unto Him who died and rose again.

> "*Love so amazing, so divine*
> *Demands my soul, my life, my all.*"

Encouragement for Closing Days

SCRIPTURES READ:
MALACHI 3:13-4:6; LUKE 1:5-6; 2:25-38

In the Book of Malachi, we get an insight as to the moral state of the remnant of Jews that returned to Jerusalem from the captivity in Babylon. We do not find that they rise to the height of their privileges, in their restored position, but lapse into a low moral state of departure and discouragement. This shows that even in a restored position, God's people can fail to appropriate the mercy and goodness of God extended to them, and grievously fail; hence the need of encouragement for the true-hearted. Though the Temple was re-built, and priestly service was restored, it appeared to them to be a vain thing to serve God. To keep His ordinance and walk before Him was no easy task, especially in circumstances where evil prevailed. All around, there were those who wrought wickedness, and even tempted God, and, to all appearance, such were delivered! In such circumstances, how easy to cease to bear witness to the truth and to abandon the position they had taken.

But, just at that time, when things were at their worst, there were those who feared the Lord. They thought upon His name. They spoke of Him one to another. In this way, they were kept by Him in an evil day. Their safety was in fearing Him; their comfort was in thinking of His name; their fellowship was in speaking of Him one to another. And to show His appreciation of them, the Lord says, they will be His in the day when He will make up His jewels. He will also reward them for their faithful service, when due discrimination will be made between him that serves God and him that serves Him not. Precious words of comfort! How they ought to stimulate us!

Then in chapter 4 we have the two unvarying principles which God lays down for the guidance of His faithful people in a day of declension and ruin. (1) They have to look forward to the Coming of Christ. (2) They have to return to what was given at the beginning; namely, the law of Moses, which God gave at Horeb. On the one hand, they had the assurance God would fulfil all His purposes for their blessing at the advent of Christ; on the other, they had the sure and infallible Word of God to which to turn for instruction as to their walk and service. So that, while they rejoiced in hope, waiting for "the consolation of Israel", they gave diligence to fulfil all that was commanded them at the beginning, without lowering the divine standard, or attempting to accommodate divine oracles to a human condition of weakness and failure.

As to hope, they looked *forward*; as to faithfulness, they went *back*—forward to the advent of Christ, when all would be consummated to the glory of God and the blessing of His people; back to what was originally set up by God, which could not alter, and which demanded the unqualified obedience of His people, whatever might be their condition of weakness and failure. And since divine principles never change, whatever be the dispensation, it goes without saying all this has an application to-day.

Coming now to the opening chapters of Luke's Gospel we get a very beautiful picture of the faithful remnant when the Lord came to His people. Three persons are outstanding in it: Zacharias, Simeon and Anna. They were all advanced in years, weak in themselves, and divested of everything in which flesh might glory. What marked them was their faithfulness to God by obedience to His word, and their earnest looking for the coming of Christ. In fact, Simeon had it revealed to him by the Holy Ghost, that he would not see death before he had seen the Lord's Christ (Jehovah's Anointed). This would show how imminent Christ's advent was to them, at the same time, how weak they were in themselves, as they waited for it. Their condition was well in keeping with what Isaiah had predicted centuries before, namely, God gave power to the faint, and increased strength to him that had no might. They waited on the Lord, and He renewed their strength (Isaiah 40:28-31).

We might say that the feature Zacharias presents to us is *faithfulness*. He and his wife Elizabeth "were both righteous before God, walking in all the commandments and ordinances of the Lord blameless." He did not follow with the current of things around him, in a path of declension and unfaithfulness, but adhered to God's word with a fidelity that is spoken of as blameless. Nor are we to suppose his lot was cast in easy circumstances. It was the close of the dispensation, when things had assumed their worst form, and to pursue the path of faithfulness against the sweeping current called for the energy of faith. To be faithful to God, in a day when all bespeaks unfaithfulness and dishonour to Him, is a singular privilege which we might all covet.

Simeon gives us the two features of *devotion* and *righteousness*. It is written of him, that he was "just and devout". Nothing is said of what he *did*, beyond the fact he waited for the consolation of Israel. We are simply told what he *was*, a devout and just man, who waited for the advent of Christ. He seems to be marked more by his *life* than by his *service*. To live devotedly and righteously before God is no small thing, when all hope is gone except that of Christ's return. All the weakness of old age had fallen upon him; his inability to take part in the activities of life had forced him into retirement; yet his life shone out in devotion and righteousness before God, and his fervent expectation of Christ's coming was rewarded, in that he saw the Lord and took "Him up in his arms".

Should we not to-day seek to live devotedly and righteously, and ardently long for Christ's return? Various reasons might prevent us from joining in active service for the Lord; but no possible reason can be alleged for not living devotedly and righteously before Him, and longing earnestly for His return.

Anna was a widow of great age, who "departed not from the temple, but served God with fastings and prayers night and day." She was a prophetess, and had the mind of the Lord about His people, and prayed for them continually. The same spirit we see in Samuel, when he said to Israel, after they had sinned, "God forbid that I should sin against the Lord in ceasing to pray for you" (1 Samuel 12:23). The temple was the proper, anointed place to pray (as 2 Chronicles 6 shows), and Anna abode by it, and sought God's ear in it, according to His Word.

In the days when this faithful widow abode by the temple, and continued to fast and pray, vendors of sheep and oxen and changers of money had turned that holy place into an "house of merchandise". How she managed to continue her devotional practices in the midst of such disorder, is marvellous; but her faith rose above the failure of the people, and rested in the faithfulness of God. God had not abandoned His house; His name was still there, notwithstanding the evil that had been brought into it; and she, faithful to Him, persevered in prayer in it.

What an incentive to prayer we have here! But how often we complain and murmur about the difficulties, instead of making prayers, intercessions, and giving of thanks, for all men, as we have been enjoined of God in 1 Timothy 2! We do well to turn from the complaining spirit, which can only lead to despondency, and give ourselves to earnest, continual, believing prayer, as did Anna.

Then it should be observed, that our position as Christians is very much higher than that of the Jews. We form the Church of God, His House through the Spirit. We are the Body of Christ, who is the Head in heaven. What untold fulness there is in Him! This fulness is available for us now, as it has always been right down through the Church's history. Having the presence and power of the Holy Spirit, and union with Christ, the Head, in heaven, we can rise above failure and avail ourselves of our high and holy privileges.

The great concern of the Apostle Paul in his ministry to, and prayer for, the saints of God, was to raise them to the height of their privileges. See his prayers in Ephesians 1 and 3. He knew the danger of the Church losing the sense of her union with Christ, the Head, and becoming occupied with things of earth. And alas! how true it is, the Church, as a whole, has lost the sense of her union with Christ, the Head in heaven, and become allied to the world in an unholy relationship, the fruit of which can only meet sure and certain judgment. But there are faithful ones who cleave to God to-day, just as there were faithful ones who cleaved to God in the Jewish dispensation, and it is such we would seek to encourage in these last and closing days.

"An Everlasting Light"

SCRIPTURES READ:
GENESIS 1:3; 2 CORINTHIANS 3:18; 4:3-6;
ISAIAH 60:1, 19-20; ACTS 26:13

I think these Scriptures speak for themselves, so I shall not occupy much time. What is before me is the fact that we have been called out of darkness into God's marvellous light.

Every Christian here can surely remember when Christ met him on the way, and light from heaven shone into his heart. Of course, we did not have conversions of the special sort that Saul of Tarsus had, but we all had been walking in darkness. In that moral darkness we remained until God shined in our hearts, to give us the light of the knowledge of the glory of God in the face of Jesus Christ. It was the God, who caused light to shine in creation, that did this.

I think we all remember the blessed moment when Christ met us on the way—the Christ who said, "I am the Light of the world"—and shining into our hearts, we discovered how dark we were. Now the sun has risen upon us, shining brighter and brighter unto the perfect day. But while we wait for the perfect day, the world has nothing but sunset before it and the darkness of night.

The Lord met me in a dense forest in Washington, America, and showed me, a young man, the darkness I was in. He showed me I was not able to meet God in my sin. Then I caught sight of the sun which shall never go down, and the Lord became to me an everlasting light, as the prophet said. What grace for each one of us when the Lord shone upon us and we came out of the darkness into the light!

Now I would go one step further for us Christians. In Psalm 43, we read, "O send out Thy light and Thy truth: let them lead me". That shows us what the Lord wants. If we are led by the light we shall be *obedient* to it. We do not need to ask the Lord so much to give us more light, but to be obedient to the light which He has given us. If we are obedient to the light that has shone into our hearts, He will lead and guide us further. Then we shall know how to behave ourselves in the house of God.

It is a wonderful story, in Acts 12 how Peter was liberated to go on with God's testimony. He was bound with chains, guarded by soldiers, and the iron door was locked. That is how the enemy would like to have us—chained, so that we do not serve the Lord. Now an angel came in with a light, and told Peter to rise. Peter might have said, "Do you not see the chains; how do you expect me to rise?" But Peter was obedient, he rose up in that light, and the chains fell off. The angel said, "Bind on thy sandals." He did so, and without hesitation he followed the angel and the light, and was delivered from the prison. When they came to the iron door it opened, and out he was able to go.

"THE EPISTLE OF CHRIST"

Where did he go? Not to the temple, that God had forsaken, but to the house of Mary, where the church was praying. Is it not wonderful that the Lord has a place for us to-day—the house of God is here. Oh, that we may be led to the place where the Lord would have us, where two or three are gathered together unto His Name. We have such wonderful experiences in Switzerland! The mountains are round about us, and the hearts of the people are naturally as hard as the rocks; yet He is working in some of these hearts and gathering some out of darkness unto Himself.

When Saul of Tarsus saw a great light above the brightness of the sun and met with the Lord of glory, from that moment he was changed—he was spoiled for this world. May the Lord so bless us that the glory of Christ may shine into our souls, and we may apprehend that for which He has apprehended us. Things are made very plain to us if we have Christ before us, not only as our Saviour but as our Priest and our Head.

Ten lepers went seeking for the priest, and as they went they were cleansed. But only one of them really found the Priest, and that was by returning to Christ. It is glorious when we find Him like that.

Christ too is the Head, and if we lay hold of Him as such, He will deliver us from all that is merely of man, and attach us to Himself. Thus He will lead us until He comes.

Unity from Above

SCRIPTURES READ:
PSALM 133; 1 THESSALONIANS 1:5-10;
1 CORINTHIANS 11:1; 2 TIMOTHY 3:1-5, 10-12

Psalm 133, a short psalm of but three verses, indicates a truth of the very first magnitude. There is a very great call nowadays for unity amongst God's people, and this Psalm indicates that *all real unity comes from above*. It gives a very interesting illustration of it. It speaks of Aaron, the High Priest of Israel, and the precious ointment, poured upon his head and beard, descending to the skirts of his garments. It is surely a very charming illustration of the Lord Jesus Christ on high, shedding forth the Holy Spirit upon all believers—the youngest and the oldest—exerting a divine influence, outside of which there can be no true unity among God's people.

It is good to emphasize that unity only comes *from above, from Christ Himself.* There may be, and alas! is, a great deal of divergence about ecclesiastical matters, but there is one thing that is absolutely vital, and that is contact with the Lord Himself, and one thing is wanted to-day, and that is Divine power, and that can only be where room is made for God and His Word. It is not sufficient to correctly understand certain doctrines, but hearts must be under the living influence of the Word and the Holy Spirit, before we can be drawn to the Lord, and to each other, and walk in Divine unity.

It may be that you wonder what connection our succeeding chapters have with Psalm 133. There is a connection, however, that speaks to us very definitely as individual Christians, for it is only as we are right *individually* that we can be right *collectively*.

The Apostle Paul wrote to the Thessalonian believers, "Our Gospel came not unto you in Word only, but also in power, and in the Holy Ghost, and in much assurance; ... and ye became followers of us and of the Lord." What an extraordinary phrasing—"followers *of us and of the Lord*"—putting himself and his companion in front of the Lord. Why should they be put in that order? It seems strange on first reading. We may disabuse our minds at the outset that Paul was a conceited man. He was very humble-minded. Why then did he say, "Ye became followers of us and of the Lord"?

There is a real reason for this. You will have to put yourselves in the shoes of those early Christians to understand the position. Imagine that you live in Thessalonica; you have been brought up in all the blackness of paganism and idolatry. One day there comes into your city the Apostle Paul, and a companion. They come without any introduction or committee behind them. They have no Bible and no hymn book. Christianity is not a continuation of Judaism. It is something fresh, and those early Christians were dependent upon what they heard and what they saw in the deportment of the preachers. When these heathen listeners were brought under the power of the Gospel and became Christians, they might say to themselves, How can I have any idea of what Christianity really is, or of what Christ is like? The only chance we have of knowing what Christ is like is by watching carefully the lives of the men who brought the good news. They would look at them very carefully, their lives would impress them, and they would imitate their ways, and they would thus become followers of the Apostle, and really of the Lord. And, if they become followers of the Lord through the Apostle in an *intermediate* way, it would lead to the following of the Lord in a very *immediate* way. That is why I read 1 Corinthians 11:1. That states the whole matter in a nutshell. All Paul wanted was that they should so see Christ in his ways, that they would follow the Lord Himself.

An illustration may help. About forty-one years ago two brothers, known to most of us, went to Central Africa and pitched their tent amongst the native inhabitants. They did not know what sort of treatment they would get, but sat down in the midst of these people, not knowing their language, and the natives not knowing theirs. They learnt their language, and began to preach the Gospel to them. These people had no Bible, they were dependent on the two brothers for any idea of what Christ was like.

Nowadays, we have our hymn books, we have our Bibles. Things are very different to-day. That is just what I want to come to; for things in reality are not *vitally* different. It has often been said very truly that we Christians read our *Bibles*, and the worldings read *us*. It makes a very searching question as to how far we are really exhibiting Christ in our lives.

2 Timothy 3:1-5, 10-12 teaches us the lesson that doctrine and practice should go together. The one thing, which is wanted to-day is *power* — power not merely with

our tongues, but power in our lives. You will remember that when the Apostle John was writing to the children of God, he said, "I write unto you young men because ye are strong, and the word of God abideth in you." That is not just reading the Bible and memorizing it, not merely getting hold of the Scriptures in the mind, but it is the Scriptures getting hold of us in our lives.

Now the Apostle Paul is set forth as a pattern saint; the Spirit of God took him and held him, so that he should be the one we should mark and learn, so that we should get our eye on Christ. Paul wanted to be a stepping stone *to Christ*.

He says, "Thou hast fully known my doctrine, manner of life." Here lies the difficulty with many of us. We have doctrine. By God's grace to us, we have got light from the Scriptures in a very full way. We have plenty of doctrine, plenty of teaching. All this may be said without boasting and in humility for it is really a searching admission. I want everyone here to put himself alongside this test — *"doctrine and MANNER OF LIFE."*

Some people say it does not matter what doctrine you hold; behaviour is everything. But, as a matter of fact, people take their character from the doctrine they believe. Wrong belief can never produce right behaviour. It is a very great thing to see this. Can I say, I have got this teaching, please observe my manner of life? Does my manner of life correspond with the teaching? It is a very searching question, and you may say we do not need it because we have the Scriptures, *but we need it as much as ever*.

We want the individual to be right, for if the individual is right the company will be helped. This is where Psalm 133 comes in. If we are right with the Lord, if we are walking in the Spirit, if the ointment descends from Aaron's head, to the skirts of his garment, then all is blessed and happy. If I do not know how to behave myself as an individual, I shall certainly not know how to walk aright with the company.

May I appeal to the young Christians here? You are young, life is opening up before you, you will have temptations that older ones have not. What opens up before you is alluring and seductive, but if you have a set purpose, and put first things first—not thinking that domestic or business affairs are the most important things in life—Christ first in everything, you will not be the loser, but the gainer by far. May this be so with each one of us.

The Cross of Christ

SCRIPTURES READ:
ROMANS 6:6; 1 CORINTHIANS 1:23-24; 2:4-8;
GALATIANS 2:19-20; 6:14-15

The last scripture, read by the previous speaker, alluded to the Apostle Paul, his doctrine and his manner of life. I am glad that my theme fits in exactly with those two things. I have read four passages, and in those from Romans and Corinthians we get summarized something of the Apostle's doctrine concerning the Cross of Christ. In Galatians we discover the working out of the doctrine, the way it affected his manner of life.

We may discriminate thus:— the first and second scriptures are *doctrinal* and *dogmatic*. They state certain things that have been divinely accomplished in the Cross of Christ. The third and fourth from Galatians are *experimental* and *practical*. You will notice that in these Galatian passages the Apostle drops from the plural into the singular and uses the little pronoun "I" a number of times; that is because he is not expounding Christian doctrine, but is showing us something of Christian experience as wrought out in himself. In this way he lets us into the secret of the marvellous manner of life that characterized him.

But what characterized him as a pattern saint is also to characterize us. The Cross of Christ is as central and as valid for us as for him. If we speak of it for a few minutes tonight we must do so with the shadow of it lying upon our spirits. Its deep significance must come closely home to us all—especially the speaker. We must learn its lesson; it is one that we have never done with while down here.

The Cross was death; but it was a death of utter repudiation, a death of degradation and shame. I think I am right in saying that it was a way of executing the death sentence introduced by the haughty Romans. They had an iron empire beside which even the British Empire is a fragile affair, and for centuries their empire existed. As you know, unspeakable cruelties were perpetrated, and when they defeated and captured poor barbarians they nailed them up in contempt, just as a farmer might nail vermin to his barn door.

This was the contemptuous treatment meted out by the Romans to their enemies; they would not give them a decent execution under the axe—that was reserved for the condemned Roman—they nailed them with supreme cruelty to a cross of wood. Now that was the death which the Lord of glory died—a death of repudiation, degradation, condemnation.

Many things might be said as to Romans 6:6, but I am going to concentrate on one. We have the dogmatic assertion that in the Cross of our Saviour our old man was crucified with Him. God *did* it. God *says* it. We *know* it, because God has said it.

Now what is the significance of "our old man"? Our "old man" is all that we were in character, as children of Adam, *personified*. It is no unusual thing for us to personify a certain character. Visualizing a man of that character, we can see more clearly what the character is.

Now scientific experiments seem to show us increasingly that there are many hidden features and potentialities in any given species, whether of animals or plants. No one specimen exhibits all the features of the species. That is equally true with men. No one man expresses all that is in man. To-day we have the Adamic race, having run perhaps through two hundred generations, and numbering roundly two thousand million; so we begin to see working out in humanity all the features that were in Adam, when as a fallen man he became the progenitor of the human race.

As I went down to the city on the first day here, I saw facing me a poster on which were the words in very large type, "Aren't men beasts!" (I might say, in passing, that the bill-poster, perhaps by a happy accident, had put close to it another poster, also in large type, reading, "The Son of Man is come to seek and to save that which was lost", and this was most appropriate). Now this remark had not got a note of interrogation following it, as though we were invited to express our opinion on the point. It had a note of exclamation. It was a bold assertion; and we have to admit, too sadly true.

All I have to say is: if you really could produce a man who should embody in himself every evil thing that ever has been displayed in the Adamic race, you would have indeed a beast—a terrible monster. There would be no peace or safety until he was condemned and executed. Well, thanks be to God, that is exactly what has been done. God has put the sentence of death on our old man—on all that we were as children of Adam. The marvellous thing is that this sentence should have been made effective in the crucifixion of our Lord Jesus Christ. He came down into death that He might take up the judgment that belongs to a man of that character, and in His Cross our old man has been crucified. That is a dogma which, when it gets into our hearts, will profoundly affect our lives.

Now in Corinthians you again have the Cross of Christ. Paul evangelized these very learned folk, who had an outward culture covering much inward corruption. He tells how he determined amongst them to know nothing save Christ crucified. Now Christ crucified is the power of God and the wisdom of God, and we see in this passage that though foolishness *to* men, it simply proves the foolishness *of* men. It is the princes of this world who stand judged in the light of the Cross, for none of them knew the Divine wisdom; had they known it they would not have crucified the Lord of glory.

With all their earthly wisdom they crucified the Lord of glory. They put His title in three languages over His head: in Latin, the language of the military and governmental princes; in Greek, the language of the intellectual princes, and in Hebrew, the language of the religious princes. All were united, Jew and Gentile. Why did they crucify the Lord of glory? Because they did not know Him. Well, if their wisdom did not enable them to recognize their Creator when they saw Him, it stands condemned.

Isaiah, in his day, said, "The ox knoweth his owner, and the ass his master's crib, but Israel doth not know." That word might now be said with far greater emphasis. Jesus the Son of God was amongst them. Did they know Him? They did not. They had not the sense of an ass!

The Lord of creation stooped in grace amongst us, and His crucifixion put the sentence of condemnation upon the world and its princes. The issue is clear cut. They crucified Him of course, but as God and the holy angels saw it, *they crucified themselves.*

There is a story told of one of the newly rich, really a very ignorant man, who went into an Art Gallery containing celebrated pictures of great value. He turned to an attendant saying, "Are these your noted pictures? I don't think much of them." The man replied, "Sir, the worth of our pictures is amply assured: they are not on their trial. It is the visitors who are on their trial." By his remark condemning the pictures, the man was really condemning *himself.* He only displayed his own foolishness and ignorance. The princes of this world condemned themselves in this fashion.

So the wisdom of the world stands condemned. This is dogmatically stated here; but now we must come to the application, for that is what we want to reach. The truth must affect us in an experimental and practical fashion, and if it does, the effect will be that we shall live unto God. The whole current and direction of our lives will be changed. There will be a new object before us. Galatians shows us this.

In our unconverted days self was at the very centre of our thinking; it was the dirty little puddle into which all our trickling streams emptied themselves. Now the stream of our life is no longer to run into the mud-pool of self; it is to flow into the glorious ocean—Christ Himself. God is to be the Object of life to the Christian; even as Paul said, "I am dead to the law, that I might live unto God."

"I" occurs no less than seven times in verses 19 and 20, and some of you may feel a little difficulty about them. There is I myself, the living entity, the individual person; but then I may sometimes identify myself in thought with what I am as a new creation in Christ Jesus, and sometimes with what I am as a child of Adam.

With this before us, let us read verse 20 again:— I—as a child of Adam—am crucified with Christ: nevertheless I—the individual person— live; yet not I—as a child of Adam—but Christ liveth in me; and the life which I—the individual person—now live in the flesh, I—the new creation man—live by the faith of the Son of God, who loved me and gave Himself for me. I was identified with Him in His death, and captivated by His mighty love, I accept as regards myself, as regards the flesh and its motions, the crucifixion that took place with Christ my Lord. Crucifixion brought home inwardly, privately, to the individual conscience and heart, so that Christ may now come out in the life: this is what accounted for the manner of life that characterized the Apostle Paul.

You probably know the old illustration about a man conscripted to serve in Napoleon's army, but being a married man, an unmarried friend took his place. After some time the substitute died in battle, and a further conscription taking place, the original man was again called up. When he did not put in an appearance he was challenged, but he stated what had happened and said that he had died in the person of his substitute.

But there was a sequel to this which you may not have heard. The matter was referred to Napoleon, who decided in his favour, saying his legal position was unassailable, but that he could not have it both ways. He could not claim to be legally dead in the person of his substitute, and yet go on living *as before*. He decreed that he must change his name. Both he and his family had henceforth to live in the name of the man who died for him. That illustrates my point, but with us it has to go much deeper than a mere change of *name*. There has to be a change of *life*—"Christ liveth in me!" The One who died—the One in whom crucifixion was an actuality—that One is now going to live in those for whom He died.

All life must have an object, and we have an adequate Object for the new life into which we are introduced in the One who loved us and gave Himself for us. For ever our eyes will be centred on Him. To-day we live by the *faith* of the Son of God. Presently we shall live by the *sight* of Him.

How amazing this is! Jesus the Son of God loved me, and gave Himself for me. The Lord of glory on the one hand, and then poor little me on the other—not merely little, but degraded, dirty, unlovely. Paul had to endorse the description of the Cretians as always liars, evil wild beasts, lazy gluttons; but then he went on to say to Titus that we ourselves were hateful and hating one another. It is as easy as anything to hate somebody else, as seeing their bad points, but we have to face the fact that we are hateful ourselves. Have you ever sat down and said, "I am a hateful person." If you have not said it, it is time you did so. Yet the Son of God looked down upon hateful me and He loved me. This is a fact that moves the heart! About the most astounding thing I know is that *He loved me when there was nothing in me to love*, and He gave Himself for me. What a melting fact is this! How gladly then do I say, "Lord Jesus, let Thy Cross lie upon that which I am, that there may be something of Thy life manifested in me."

Now as I close, one word about the world. Its wisdom comes to nothing, as Corinthians tells us. The world itself comes to nothing. John tells us that—"The world passeth away, and the lust thereof." The Apostle Paul in our passage, again speaks personally and experimentally saying,

"God forbid that I should glory, save in the Cross of our Lord Jesus Christ." He gloried in that sentence of repudiation, shame and death. That Cross stood between Paul and the world, for not only was the world crucified unto him but he to the world.

I wonder which of those two things is the more difficult for us to take in. Has the world died a shameful death of repudiation in our eyes? Has the death of Christ torn the gaudy mask from the face of the world? She is not a lovely damsel: she is a wrinkled old hag. Have we seen its true character as tested by the presence of the Lord of glory?

But then, the world says, "I don't want you. You are crucified in my eyes." Now it is a very humiliating thing thus to be crucified to the world. Paul found it so; the sentence of the Cross was upon him; and yet he said, God forbid that I should glory in anything else but this.

May God help us to look at things in this light, and may the Cross of Christ stand between us and the world. May we glory in the Cross, even as Paul did. How much did the Cross cost our Saviour? What did it mean to Him?

Many centuries ago the custom crept in of wearing or carrying crucifixes, which, it was thought, would remind people of the Cross of Christ. Very soon the reality was lost. The symbol killed the reality it was supposed to keep alive. What we want is that the Cross, in its real significance may really lie engraven upon the fleshy tables of our hearts.

Lord and Christ

SCRIPTURES READ: GENESIS 41:37-40;
MATTHEW 12:15-21; ACTS 2:33-36;
1 CORINTHIANS 1:1-3; 2 CORINTHIANS 1:19-22

My message is in relation to the Headship and Lordship of Christ; that we may consider, first, the blessing secured for the saints of God in Him who is raised from among the dead and glorified at God's right hand; then, as the result of our being blessed in Him as Head, the obligation, as well as the great privilege, of being subject to Him as our Lord.

We may well give special attention to these two thoughts in these last days of the church's history on earth, when in her responsibility she has very apparently failed. We may well give thanks to God that in these days of weakness and failure the same grace and guidance are available for us, as in the early days of the church. Thus a way is open for the overcomer; that is, for any who will avail themselves of the grace given, to enjoy the blessings and answer to the obligations.

I have read the verses in Genesis 41 so that we may see in Joseph *typically* what we have *really* in Christ. As with the Lord Jesus, so it was with Joseph, humiliation and rejection preceded exaltation. Joseph came, as sent by his father, to enquire as to the welfare of his brethren, but was met by their hatred and sold by them into Egypt. The Spirit of God records that with Joseph three things went down into Egypt, spicery, balm, and myrrh. We see the beauty of this only as we view by faith Him who is greater than Joseph. The spicery would surely tell us of the fragrance of the perfect life of the Lord Jesus. He did always the things that pleased the Father and which could be fully appreciated only by the Father. The balm would set forth the healing power and grace offered to man and available to everyone in need. The myrrh would set forth the sorrow which was ever His portion down here as the "Man of sorrows" in a world of sin and grief. Thus, in the type, we see that if Joseph is sent into Egypt the blessing must go with him. Until his brethren come to where he is, their history is one of failure and famine.

Our thoughts revert to Matthew 23:38-39, where we see the Lord Jesus rejected by His earthly people, leaving the temple for the last time, and we hear Him saying: "Behold your house is left unto you desolate; for I say unto you, Ye shall not see me henceforth till ye shall say, Blessed is He that cometh in the name of the Lord." In the passage we read, in chapter 12, the Pharisees were counselling to destroy Him, while He Himself (now in seclusion) was still going on with His works of goodness, and God was inviting those who had ears to hear and anointed eyes, to behold the beauty of His Servant, in whom His soul delighted.

The passage from Isaiah 42 quoted in Matthew 12 closes with the words, "In Him shall the Gentiles trust." In verse 37 of our chapter in Genesis we read, "The thing was good in the eyes of Pharaoh, and in the eyes of his servants." These words show that our hearts are to be engaged with Him who was ever God's delight, and that the One who was rejected and crucified here, has been made Lord and Christ. To Joseph, Pharaoh addresses the words, "Thou shalt be over my house and according to thy word shall all my people regulate themselves" (N.Tr.). Joseph was not only a dreamer of dreams, he was also the interpreter of dreams and the fulfiller of them.

I have thought that the words "Thou shalt be over my house" might be considered in the light of the truth brought before us in 2 Corinthians. Our hearts are there set at rest through being engaged with the Son of God, Jesus Christ, in whom all the promises of God are eternally verified.

In Psalm 36 we read: "They shall be abundantly satisfied with the fatness of Thy house; and Thou shalt make them drink of the river of Thy pleasures." Through the work of redemption accomplished on the Cross, God can now bless man according to His own purpose and grace. Christ's place in the glory is the pattern and pledge to all who put their trust in Him. Of course we must always bear in mind that in all things He must have pre-eminence. The Spirit of God who indwells each believer is the anointing, the seal, and the earnest of all our blessings. In Ephesians 3 we find the apostle saying, "Unto me, who am less than the least of all saints, is this grace given, that I should preach among the Gentiles the unsearchable riches of Christ." The Gospel of the Glory, then, as committed to Paul, brings before us in a special way God's thoughts of blessing for all who believe on His Son during this present day of grace. Believers are blessed with all spiritual blessings in heavenly places in Christ.

The Headship of Christ is viewed in various aspects in Scripture: 1 Corinthians 11:3; Ephesians 1:10, 22;

Colossians 1:18; 2:10. The prominent thought seems to be derivation. If it be the saints to-day, or the redeemed creation in the coming day, all are to derive from, and take character from Him who is Head. But if through sovereign grace all our blessings are eternally secured in our risen and exalted Head, there are also present obligations resting upon us as the result of these blessings being ours.

This brings us to the second part of our verse in Genesis 41: "According to thy word shall all my people be ruled." May we not apply these words to the main teaching of 1 Corinthians, where we have the Lordship of Christ prominently brought before us? The world has expressed its thought of the Son of God in the words, "Away with Him, crucify Him." God has given His answer to this in making Him Lord and Christ. We find it stated in Acts 10:36. "He is Lord of all." This is not yet publicly manifested.

We may briefly consider the Lordship of Christ in a threefold aspect. First, in relation to believers individually, as in 1 Corinthians 6, "Ye are not your own for ye are bought with a price: therefore glorify God in your body." The body is for the Lord and the Lord for the body. We do well to pause here and challenge ourselves in this manner, "Is the Lord Jesus, the One whom the world refuses, the One into whose hands God has committed all things, controlling and guiding me in every detail of my life?" His claims upon us are claims of love. May we ever say from the heart, "Lord we are Thine, Thy claims we own."

Secondly, we have the collective sphere where His Lordship is to be maintained in 1 Corinthians 12 and 14. In the great house of profession, we see everywhere human organization. While the Lord's name is professed, God's word, and the divine order set forth therein, are ignored or refused. Is there then a possibility of yielding to Him His rights in this collective way? Surely there is. The instructions given in 1 Corinthians 12 are obligatory on us to-day in spite of the outward breakdown of the church. This was surely anticipated by the Lord Jesus when He promised that "Where two or three are gathered together in My name there am I in the midst of them." If there has been failure, and if there is but little strength, surely there is still an open door for faithfulness. The new cart, setting forth human arrangement, might be tolerated amongst the Philistines, but not amongst the people of God. See 1 Samuel 6:7, and 2 Samuel 6:3-7.

Finally, the full extent of the Lordship of Christ will be manifested when He shall have put down all rule, and authority, and power, and shall deliver up the kingdom of God, even the Father, that God may be all in all, as we see in 1 Corinthians 15.

May it be ours through grace, while waiting for His coming, to be rejoicing in the blessings He has won for us, and gladly owning His claims upon us in every sphere, saying from our hearts:—

> "Thee we reverence, Thee obey,
> Own Thee Lord and Christ alway."

The Path of Obedience

SCRIPTURES READ:
REVELATION 1:10-11; JOHN 21:22;
1 CORINTHIANS 1:10; EPHESIANS 4:3;
1 TIMOTHY 3:15-16; 3 JOHN 13-14

From these scriptures I desire to say a few words, with the Lord's help and the encouragement of my brethren, as to the position and outlook of faith. Most of us here recognize the ruin of the public testimony entrusted to the church, and I want to differentiate between that and the present path of obedience that lies before us.

In Revelation 1, John has his back upon the church, and the voice he hears recalls him to it in the form of seven assemblies—a fallen and falling church, as it has been said. There is revealed a state of things only permitted to continue by the Lord since He, as Son of Man, is scrutinizing and judging all that is there, whilst encouraging too. The earliest phase of the church, formed under Peter's ministrations, passed away in the destruction of Jerusalem; that under Paul's had failed, for he had to say, "All seek their own, not the things which are Jesus Christ's" (Philippians 2:21). The address to the church at

"THE EPISTLE OF CHRIST"

Thyatira shows that there is no return to the original estate, and only the coming of Christ is looked for.

Now there must be a thorough bowing under the governmental hand of God. The Lord's verdict as to Philadelphia was that there was but a little strength, and there must be a bowing as to this; for I am assured that if more is attempted than a little strength warrants, we shall but drop into organization. What then, have we to-day? It is to answer this that I have read the Lord's statement to Peter in John 21.

Peter had said, "I will" to the Lord (John 13:37), and how had it ended? In his thrice denying Him. And that is how our "I will" works out. Now, the Lord says to him, "If I will that he abide until I come, what is that to thee? Follow *thou* Me" (N.Tr.). There is that which does not fail, but stands in the "I will" of Christ. I take it that all that is precious and pleasing to God to-day subsists along that line.

Does not that put our hearts in a true position before God? I take courage from the sense of His gracious faithfulness to us in our low estate. Our responsibility is maintained in the "Follow Me", but the Divine sovereignty runs through all—the "I will" of Christ. So too, in 2 Timothy 2, the Divine sovereignty is strongly marked in, "The Lord knoweth them that are His"; as our responsibility is disclosed in, "Let every one that nameth the name of the Lord depart from iniquity."

Now 1 Corinthians views the church as witness to the Lordship of Christ, as our dear brother has just been saying to us; and it is here where particularly the breakdown in the public testimony is evidenced. Does a popular hierarchy and priesthood meet the case? Does an official oversight in a system of local independent assemblies?

Does that not all the rather evidence a denial of the ruin? A meeting is formed by the preaching of the truth. What then has it for guidance but this very Epistle? It is not a matter of testimony, but of obedience.

Any testimony since apostolic days has been but a fitful flash which illuminated for a moment a mighty but ruined structure: but we are never absolved from the necessity of *obedience*. Are we, for instance, to avoid full obedience to the injunctions of chapter 5, and turn for guidance to 2 Timothy 2? 2 Timothy is not an ecclesiastical Epistle, but guidance to a man of God. Then these "diversities of gifts" and of service, of which chapters 12-14 speak; are we to give all this up and substitute a clergy? The Lord preserve us from it!

So too Ephesians. By divine teaching we know we are formed into "one new man", "one body", that through Christ we have "access by one Spirit unto the Father", that we are an "habitation of God through the Spirit"; and we may have Christ dwelling in the heart by faith; then we are exhorted to use diligence to keep the unity of the Spirit. In 1 Corinthians we are commanded by the Name of our Lord Jesus Christ to be united (1:10). "He that hath My commandments, and keepeth them, he it is that loveth Me" (John 14:21). Does that only apply to what John records? It applies to *every word* of the Lord; and the test of love is obedience.

Then there is the gospel. But the gospel goes out from the house of God, where the Saviour-God dwells, who desires all men to be saved and come to a knowledge of the truth. The church does not teach but is taught, and then it supports and displays the truth, as a "pillar" (1 Timothy 3:15). Hence personal piety is enjoined on the men and women who form that house, and the secret of it is this—

"God was manifest in the flesh, justified in the Spirit, seen of angels, preached unto the Gentiles, believed on in the world, received up into glory."

And what is the living Centre and power of all these things? Whether it be a matter of God's revelation to us or our approach to Him, Christ fills all. "Now the Lord is that Spirit" (2 Corinthians 3:17). I remember the remark of a beloved brother, that the Lord was the spirit of the Tabernacle. What is subjective and supporting is in Him, who has absolute *authority* over us. But He is *Head* to the assembly.

Then as to the "friends" (3 John 14). For long enough it did not dawn upon me that the reference is to John 15. "I call you not servants; for the servant knoweth not what his lord doeth: but I have called you friends; for all things that I have heard of My Father I have made known unto you", and again, "Ye are my friends, if ye do whatsoever I command you." The blessed and eternal Son of God has taken us out of the servant's place, and set us in this place of favour as those who obey Him. "Greet the friends by name." Precious word!

Are we cleaving to these things? When a wife loves her husband every word of his is precious to her. How then do these things stand? They stand in the Divine will and in the living affections of the heart of the saint. Sometimes there is the sense, as one views the company of God's people, "Yes, I belong to them and they belong to me" —as we all do to Christ. These divine links, there is nothing like them, is there?

It is not only "If any man love not the Lord Jesus Christ let him be Anathema Maranatha" (1 Corinthians 16:22). No, this is better—true indeed as that is—"Greet the friends by name."

THE PATH OF OBEDIENCE

"If I will that he tarry *till I come* ... follow thou Me."
"Amen. Even so, *come*, Lord Jesus" (Revelation 22:20).

Christ's Building and ours

SCRIPTURES READ: MATTHEW 16:18;
1 CORINTHIANS 3:9-15; ROMANS 15:18-21

I add a word on the scriptures which I have just read, which came forcibly to my mind as I sat listening. In the first scripture, Christ declared, "Upon this Rock, I will build My church." This wonderful statement has again and again been spoken of and we have been reminded constantly that since Christ has declared, "I *will* build", faith can rest assured that no power can thwart Him— "the gates of hell shall not prevail". He will carry all to completion and the church will at last be seen in all its perfection and glory. By the grace of God, when that day of glory dawns, we shall be there.

This Scripture, then, sets forth Christ as the great foundation Stone, and He, Himself, the Builder. Yet, from the other scriptures read, it is evident that there is that in which we too have our part as builders.

In the early part of Matthew 16 we read of how the Pharisees and Sadducees in their blind unbelief ask for a sign from heaven and Jesus, turning away from them, turns to His disciples with the enquiry, "Whom do men say that I, the Son of man, am?" Then as now all sorts of theories were being put forth as to the person of Christ, but none acknowledged His Deity.

Receiving their reply, Jesus then puts the question, "But whom say ye that I am?" This brought from Peter the glorious confession, "Thou art the Christ, the Son of the living God." How this answer must have rejoiced the Son of God, for He exclaimed, "Blessed art thou, Simon Barjona: for flesh and blood hath not revealed it unto thee, but My Father which is in heaven."

How plainly in his reply did Peter make confession of faith that Christ was the Son of Him, who is the Living One, the One who was, who is, and who is to come, the Eternal. And does not the whole incident make it plain that what matters is not so much what people in general are saying of Christ, but rather what your answer and mine is to the question, "But whom say ye that I am?" Because we cannot build aright unless we have in the faith of our souls the glad acknowledgment of the Deity of Christ. Let us each, then, in quietness, consider solemnly as in the presence of God, Christ's question, "Whom say ye that I am?"

If from your heart you can reply as Peter did, you will never give up, but will go forward with the firm assurance that Christ will bring to full fruition that to which He set His hand, when He said, "I will build My Church."

With this as the faith of our souls, we can go on to consider the other two scriptures, which relate to what *we* are building. The one says to us, "Take care what you build on the foundation"; the other, "Take care on what foundation you build." What material are we using in our building activities for the Lord? Does it consist of gold, silver, precious stones, or of wood, hay, stubble? This question is of all importance, for our scripture gives warning that, "Every man's work shall be made manifest: for the day shall declare it, because it shall be revealed by fire; and the fire shall try every man's work of what sort it is." Our work may look imposing now, but the question is, "Will it stand the test in the day of manifestation?"

The material that will stand the fire is spoken of as gold, silver, precious stones, which surely set forth divine righteousness, redemption and the glories of Christ as they were made manifest by His cross. On the other hand wood, hay, stubble will not stand the test by fire. Such material may well be described by the words of the Apostle Paul as that which is "after the commandments and doctrines of men" and "all ... to perish with the using" (Colossians 2:22). Then let us all in every activity be true to the glorious gospel of Christ, and the whole truth of God, making much of our adorable Lord and Saviour.

Lastly, let us be careful as to the foundation on which we build. To those of us who preach, invitations to address companies gathered together by others under various conditions are attractive; but, if we would build on a right foundation, may we not have to exercise care lest we build on another man's foundation, and leave souls, to whom we are blessed, to be established in that with which we ourselves could not with good conscience become allied?

But above all, what was in the mind of the Apostle was not to go where Christ was already named, but to preach the gospel to those who had never heard the good news. How Christ-like such an aim is, and how truly did Paul manifest the spirit of the true evangelist. Let us give heed to his appeal as he writes by the Holy Ghost, "Be ye followers of me, even as I also am of Christ" (1 Corinthians 11:1).

Do not let us dismiss the subject by saying that it is only in heathen lands Christ is not named and that we have no call to the heathen. For there are villages (and possibly towns) within easy reach of all of us, where there is no preaching of the clear soul-saving Gospel in which we rejoice. Can we, who have the Bread of Life, leave such to perish, because we are so taken up with our own blessings, or in fulfilling appointments to preach to ready-made companies, who have already heard the Gospel? God forbid! Rather let us find an incentive to go forward in the exhortation of Nehemiah, "Go your way, eat the fat, and drink the sweet, and send portions unto them for whom nothing is prepared" (Nehemiah 8:10). How often have I to go on my knees and pray, "O Lord, forgive me that I have so little zeal."

Let us aim at building only what is of Christ, and let us ask for the love and zeal needed to make Him known, where the Gospel is not preached. Our building activities will then be approved in the day of manifestation, to the glory of Christ.

Christ, the Object: His constraining Love, the Power

SCRIPTURES READ:
PHILIPPIANS 3:7-14; 2 CORINTHIANS 5:12-17

The first great cardinal truth is that Christ, after having accomplished redemption, has taken His seat in heaven at the right hand of God. Faith sees Him there as the glorified Man, and is attracted to Him. In fact, for faith, He is the Object supreme, that eclipses all other attractions.

The next great truth is, that the Holy Spirit has come down from heaven, and indwells all Christians individually, and the church as a whole. He unites us to Christ in the glory. His work is to reproduce the life of Christ in Christians, that there may be a continuation of His life on earth to God's glory, and the blessing of mankind.

Upon these two great truths, namely, Christ in glory, as Man, and the Holy Spirit in the church on earth, true Christianity largely rests. Of course, redemption was necessary, for man had to be redeemed, before he could be blessed. Now this presents the greatest possible contrast to the Jewish religion. Under law, the Jews were commanded to fulfil certain requirements. No power was given to them to do this. They were, consequently, thrown back on themselves, only to find they had no strength for the task, and so the law became "the ministration of death". Under grace, Christians are attracted to Christ, who has done all that was necessary for God's glory and their blessing. He has now ascended on high as the Centre of all God's counsels, having also become the Object supreme of their love, worship and service. Having Christ as Object, and the Holy Spirit as Power, Christians are transformed "from glory to glory" (2 Corinthians 3:18). This is the normal life of Christians, namely, Christ reproduced in them by the power of the Holy Spirit; they being His epistle, known and read of all men.

The life that the Apostle Paul lived on earth was but the life of Christ manifested in him. He could say, "Christ liveth in me", and again, "For to me to live is Christ." Extraordinary as this may seem, it was nevertheless true. It was his normal life. He saw Christ in glory; was attracted to Him there; and, beholding Him with unveiled face, was changed from glory to glory. Of necessity, this led to his being detached from everything on earth, in which the flesh could glory, it being eclipsed by what he saw in Christ, just as the powerful magnet in the steel works attracts the steel but leaves the dross. Surely, Christ at the right hand of God, the Object of faith, eclipses all glory on earth in man in the flesh! Hence he could say, "What things were gain to me [that is, as man in the flesh], those I counted loss for Christ."

Earthly glory is but a *hindrance* to a heavenly man. It is like the clay that sticks to one's feet and hinders one's progress. To get rid of it is no *loss*, but real *gain*; hence he esteemed the earthly glory he had left as *dung*. It was in order that he might win Christ, the Object that attracted him, the goal to which he ran in the heavenly race. May we not all follow his example?

Coming to the second part of our subject, we have the constraining love of Christ as the great power of all devoted life and service—the power in which we can live the life of Christ down here. "For the love of Christ constraineth us; because we thus judge, that if one died for all, then were all dead; and that He died for all, that they which live should not henceforth live unto themselves, but unto Him which died for them, and rose again." The greatest power that acts in the Christian is the constraining love of Christ. This love takes him away from "self", which is the centre of the old life, the selfish life, and draws him to Christ, the Centre of the new life, the unselfish life. The old life is selfishness, living *unto self*; the new life is unselfishness, living *unto Christ*. Under the power of His constraining love, we no longer live *unto ourselves*, but *unto Him*, who died and rose again.

Judaizing teachers would not only rob Christians of Christ, as the true Object for faith, but would revive in them self-love, which naturally makes self its centre. They set up man in the flesh as object, and gloried in the flesh, avoiding the cross of Christ, "lest they should suffer persecution" (Galatians 6:12-14). How differently does Christ's constraining love act in us! It leads us to glory in His Cross; accept meekly all the suffering it entails; and live unto Him who died and rose again.

So in Philippians 3 we have the *attractive* power of Christ personally: in 2 Corinthians 5, the *constraining* power of His love. Love does not live for self; it lives for others. It says, "I will very gladly spend and be spent for you; though the more abundantly I love you, the less I be loved" (2 Corinthians 12:15). It does not spend itself on others, in order to be loved by them; it gives of its own, and expects nothing in return. Let us not start saying, "*I will* do this or that: I will do better in future." That would be counting on the flesh. If drawn to Christ, these things will be produced naturally as living unto Him. Oh! to be filled with this love! The constraining love of Christ!

The Knowledge of the Son of God

SCRIPTURES READ:
EPHESIANS 1:17; 4:13; PHILIPPIANS 3:8, 10

Christianity was born at the confluence of three great civilisations. Alexander the Great in his conquest of the Orient had been the apostle of *Greek* learning, Julius Caesar and other generals had brought under *Rome's* sway a large portion of the habitable earth, while in the providence of God the *Hebrew* people had been so dispersed that Moses had in every city them that preached him being read in the synagogue every sabbath day. It was thus in the languages of culture, government and religion that the kingly glory of the Crucified was proclaimed in the superscription of His accusation.

Just a few years after the tragedy of Calvary there journeyed to Damascus a man who was the flower and fruit of these three civilisations; the scholar of Tarsus, home of philosophy, able to quote the Greek classics, the Hebrew rabbi steeped in the traditions of the fathers, and the man who could utter the magic words, "I am a Roman citizen." Then suddenly an epoch-making event took place, when his rank, breeding and religion became to him as nothing, when the proud scholar and the orthodox religionist acknowledge ignorance and unbelief—"I did it ignorantly in unbelief" (1 Timothy 1:13), and the haughty Roman surrendered with the words, "Lord, what wilt Thou have me do?" What had wrought this revolution? Nothing less than a revelation. "It pleased God, who ... called me by His grace, to reveal His Son in me" (Galatians 1:15-16). From that moment everything else was eclipsed by the surpassingness of the knowledge of Christ Jesus his Lord, and his consuming passion was to know, to preach and to magnify the Son of God.

> *Christ! I am Christ's! and let the Name suffice you,*
> *Ay, for me too He greatly hath sufficed;*
> *Lo with no winning words I would entice you,*
> *Paul has no honour and no friend but Christ.*

To this end were directed all his energies in preaching; and the purpose of ministry in the church, he tells us, is that the saints might arrive at the knowledge of the Son of God. Bacon once remarked that he took all knowledge to be his province, but we live in the days foretold by Daniel when knowledge has been so increased, that no one can devote himself to more than a small portion of things knowable. But if we know Christ, we know, in potentiality, all things, for in Him are hid all the treasures of wisdom and knowledge.

Theology, the prince of sciences, searches for the mighty Being who is the First Cause, and the simplest believer has found Him revealed in the Son of His love, "who is the image of the invisible God" (Colossians 1:15). Science explores the record of the rocks and the story of the stars for the origin of the material universe, and the child of God knows that the hand of the Saviour is that by which all things were made, visible and invisible. History delves into the past and tries to read the purpose of the ages, and the Christian knows that

> "Christ is the end, for Christ was the beginning,
> Christ the beginning, for the end is Christ."

Thus did Paul learn to know Him in His pre-incarnate glory, the glory which He had with the Father before the world was.

But he knew Him too in the mystery of His incarnation, for "when the fulness of the time was come, God sent forth His *Son* made of a woman" (Galatians 4:4), and that Holy One did not despise the Virgin's womb. Last night we shrank in horror from the picture of the "old man", and when we saw what a monstrosity the incarnation of all man's evil would be, did we not cry, "Let him be crucified"? What then shall we see and say when we come to behold God manifest in flesh, the Word become incarnate? A Babe wrapped in swaddling clothes cradled in a manger, a Boy absorbed in the things of His Father, a perfect Man doing ever those things that please the Father, whose thoughts and words and deeds provide for us a study not only for a lifetime, but for all eternity. Shall we not with shepherds, sages, saints and martyrs fall down and worship?

And when the scholar came to Corinth among the learned Greeks, what was his determination? Not to know anything among them save Jesus Christ, and Him crucified. The religionist owned himself crucified by that very law to the keeping of which his whole life had been devoted, and the proud Roman knew something of the greatest force in the universe, when he adoringly exclaimed, "the Son of God ... loved me, and gave Himself for me" (Galatians 2:20). Oh that we might know more of the Son of God in the blood-red glory of His cross, and make this our only boast!

But Paul's gospel was concerning the Son of God, who was declared, or demonstrated, to be such "with power, according to the Spirit of holiness, by the resurrection from the dead" (Romans 1:4); and his desire was to know the power of His resurrection. On that quiet Easter morning something absolutely unique in the world's history took place, a breach was made in the mighty wall of death through which there has been pouring ever since the boundless ocean of incalculable power, lifting men and women in every corner of the earth above the pollutions, pursuits, pleasures and perils of this world. The all-conquering Son of God has broken the power of the King of Terrors, the Holy One of God could not be holden of death, and He whom God raised again saw no corruption. Those who have the faith of this victorious Son of God know what it is to overcome the world.

Now this same Son of God is consecrated for evermore, a great High Priest who has passed through the heavens and sits exalted at the right hand of God. His work of sacrifice for sin having been once and for ever perfected, He now continues His service, never transferred to another, of succouring and sympathizing with His tried and tested saints who are compassed about with every kind of infirmity. How blessed to know Him in this capacity and to experience His guidance through the desert and His leading in the sanctuary.

This Son of God has also formed "the fellowship" into which God has called us by His grace (1 Corinthians 1:9). When the rebel Saul of Tarsus was converted, he received there and then a revelation of the truth that Christ and His saints are one in these words, "Why persecutest thou

Me?" and henceforth Paul the Apostle's task was to further the formation of that communion of saints, variously described in his letters as the House of God, the Body of Christ and the Bride. How precious to know we are not isolated units in this world, but have been brought into the fellowship of God's Son, and been baptised into one body by His Spirit.

When, however, we read of this glorious purpose of God for His church and then view its apparent failure and breakdown, our hearts might well be dismayed, and wonder if our hopes have been misplaced. Then comes to us Paul's assuring words, "The Son of God, Jesus Christ, who was preached among you by us ... was not yea and nay, but in Him was yea; for all the promises of God in Him are yea, and in Him Amen, unto the glory of God by us" (2 Corinthians 1:19-20); and thus we can join with the Thessalonian saints in waiting with joyful expectation for God's Son from heaven, Deliverer from the wrath to come and Completer of all God's counsels.

> *"Hark what a sound, and too divine of hearing,*
>   *Stirs on the earth and trembles in the air!*
> *Is it the thunder of the Lord's appearing?*
>   *Is it the music of His people's prayer?*
>
> *Surely He cometh, and a thousand voices*
>   *Shout to the saints and to the deaf are dumb;*
> *Surely He cometh, and the earth rejoices*
>   *Glad in His coming, who hath sworn, I come."*

What a subject for contemplation; to know Him, the Son of God in His creatorial power, His condescending grace, His cross of shame and His conquest of death; to view Him as the consecrated High Priest, as the Head of a mighty communion of saints, and as Completer of God's purpose, and to have for our blessed hope His coming again in triumph and great glory.

"The Epistle of Christ"

Scripture read: 2 Corinthians 3:2-3, 18

I have read these verses to suggest that they sum up the ministry that the Lord has so graciously given us at this time.

The outstanding thought has been, I judge, that, as believers, we have been left in this world to represent Christ. The Corinthian saints, to whom the Apostle was writing, had been using their gifts to exalt themselves before the world. But the Apostle shows that we are not left here to be great preachers, or teachers, or to make a religious reputation for ourselves, but to represent Christ —the Man that has gone to glory.

In this connection we notice three things in these verses:—

> First, the Apostle speaks of these believers as "the epistle of Christ". He does not say, "Ye *should be* the epistle of Christ", but *"Ye are"*. We are the epistle of Christ, not by anything we have done, or can do, but by the Spirit of the living God writing Christ on the heart.
>
> Secondly, these saints were not only the epistle of Christ, but, having judged the evil that had existed in

their midst, the Apostle can now say, "Ye are *manifestly declared* to be the epistle of Christ", "*known and read* of all men." We may indeed be the epistle of Christ and yet our lives so poor that nothing of Christ can be seen by the world.

Thirdly, Christ in the glory is presented as a living Person to engage our hearts. It is only as we are looking at Him that we shall become changed into the same image, and thus the writing of Christ in the heart will be kept clear and distinct.

Thus we have three great thoughts:—Christ in the heart, holding our affections; Christ in the glory, our Object; and Christ in the life, known and read of all men.

We all recall with affection the beloved brother, who was amongst the first to suggest our coming together, and whom the Lord has recently taken home to Himself. We valued his thoughtful ministry, but above all we shall cherish his memory because we saw Christ in him. I have in my study a photograph of our brother and underneath I have written the well-known lines:—

> *"For me 'twas not the truth you taught—*
> *To you so clear, to me so dim—*
> *But when you came to me you brought*
> *A sense of HIM."*

If, as the result of these meetings, we get some fresh sense of HIM, it will not be in vain that we have been together. We may not be able to take in, and retain, all the truth we have heard, but a lasting mark will be made on our souls if we can carry away some fresh impression of Christ—a sense of Him.

In closing I would like to read the 8th verse of the fifty-second chapter of Isaiah:—

> "With the voice together shall they sing: for they shall see eye to eye, when the LORD shall bring again Zion."

The prophet has looked back over the sad history of Israel and Judah, long divided by evil and strife. Then he looks on to the future and sees that the LORD is going to reign in Zion and, with the glorious vision of that day filling his soul he can prophesy of those so long divided, "with the voice together shall they sing; for they shall see eye to eye."

We too look back over the long history of the failure of the church in responsibility as a witness for Christ. But we look on and see the day of glory drawing nigh when all the strife will be for ever passed. We shall sing together, and we shall see *eye to eye*, when we see *HIM face to face*. Even now, as we look away from ourselves, and turn our thoughts to Christ in the glory, and get some fresh sense of HIM, and of His loveliness, we shall, in that measure, see eye to eye, and sing together.

Other Books by F. B. Hole
from Scripture Truth Publications

Salvation

ISBN 978-0-901860-17-0 (paperback)
211 pages; June 1998

Key Teachings

ISBN 978-0-901860-16-3 (paperback)
151 pages; June 1998

New Testament Commentary series:

The Gospels and Acts

ISBN 978-0-901860-42-2 (paperback)
ISBN 978-0-901860-46-0 (hardback)
392 pages; February 2007

Romans and Corinthians

ISBN 978-0-901860-43-9 (paperback)
ISBN 978-0-901860-47-7 (hardback)
176 pages; February 2007

Galatians to Philemon

ISBN 978-0-901860-44-6 (paperback)
ISBN 978-0-901860-48-4 (hardback)
204 pages; February 2007

Hebrews to Revelation

ISBN 978-0-901860-45-3 (paperback)
ISBN 978-0-901860-49-1 (hardback)
304 pages; February 2007

www.ingramcontent.com/pod-product-compliance
Lightning Source LLC
Chambersburg PA
CBHW031942070426
42450CB00005BA/343